CAMPING, CANINES & OTHER CANDID TALES

Life Lessons From Out and About

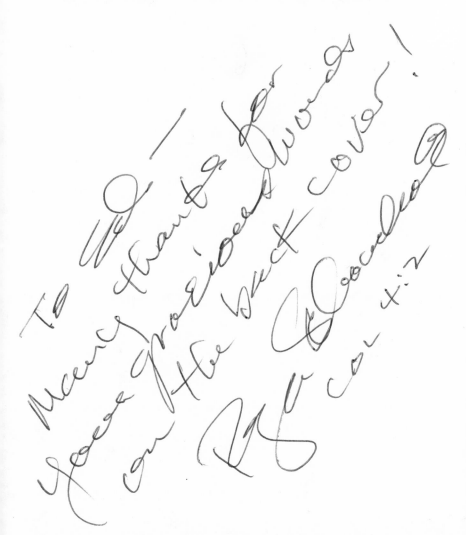

CAMPING, CANINES & OTHER CANDID TALES

Life Lessons From Out and About

G. ROGER SCHOENHALS

REDEMPTION
PRESS

Published by Redemption Press, PO Box 427, Enumclaw, WA 98022
Toll Free (844) 2REDEEM (273-3336)

Redemption Press is honored to present this title in partnership with the author. The views expressed or implied in this work are those of the author. Redemption Press provides our imprint seal representing design excellence, creative content and high quality production.

ISBN 13: 978-1-68314-236-2

Library of Congress Catalog Card Number: 2017941122

Dedication

To Jonathan, my one and only son,
a man of faith and integrity who
has been my partner in many
adventures, including several
recorded in this book.

Contents

Introduction

*C*amping, Canines & Other Candid Tales—Life Lessons From
Out and About is a collection of stories from my adventures,
mostly in the out-of-doors. The episodes are roughly arranged
according to content.

Before giving you an overlook of the chapters, I want you to
know that these stories include some of my favorite memories.
They span more than 50 years of my life and take place mostly
in the Pacific Northwest. I am confident you will enjoy them.

Also, I should point out that the grouping below is somewhat
arbitrary. For example, the section on camping does not include
every reference to camping in the book. Some of the Land
Cruiser stories also contain camping episodes. This is especially
true with the chapter titled, "Mozart and Snapping Bungees."

The first four chapters focus on camping tales, such as the
way I managed to botch our honeymoon in the wilds of Canada.

The next four chapters feature accounts involving dogs in
happy and unhappy circumstances. Either you will feel sorry for
the dog...or for me...or for both of us.

I then take you for a six-chapter ride in my two Toyota Land Cruisers. Some of these experiences are probably best left untold, especially the accounts involving my long-suffering wife. Yet I am compelled to get these memories off my chest.

Chapters 15 through 23 usher you to some sad and happy times during my early years. The title of chapter 15 reveals the underlying theme of the section: "Dumb Things I've Done." Actually, this theme seems to run through the entire book!

The final 10 chapters relate a hodgepodge of happenings during my adult years. We go from living off the grid in the wilderness, to standing in a swift-moving river, to a timeshare pitch in Orlando, Florida, to a lavish outside dinner on a ridge in Eastern Washington—and various places between. I conclude with one of my favorite stories of a two-mile race that ended in hilarious laughter.

As in my other life-lesson books, you will find that I end most of the stories with a moral or spiritual connection. I hope you consider this helpful in applying the experiences to your own life. After all, life itself is a schoolroom that teaches us about values and how to live in a worthwhile way.

In these pages you will discover honest reporting of my errors of judgment and some just plain dumb decisions. At times you may wince or laugh, or perhaps even experience a bit of inspiration. All of the stories are true.

If you enjoy these stories, you will like my other life-lesson books: *Saga of the Red Truck—Life Lessons From Here and There*; and *Hikes, Flights & Lookout Stories—Life Lessons from High Places*. You will find information about these and my other publications at www.papathree.com.

Chapter 1

How I Botched Our Honeymoon

Sandy and I were married August 15, 1964 in Ferndale, Michigan. We had a simple, sacred ceremony and the bride was extraordinarily beautiful. The honeymoon deserves attention, but not before relating the gaff I made during the actual wedding.

We were exchanging vows and I held my breath as Sandy repeated the words of the pastor. I hoped she could make it through without flubbing the lines. After all, I was a few years older and a recent seminary graduate. If there was to be a mistake, it would doubtless come from my dear bride.

She made it through perfectly and the minister turned to me and said, "Repeat after me." I stepped up to the plate, as it were, and with a commanding voice echoed the phrases directed to me, "I, Roger Schoenhals, take you, Sandra Quantrell, to be my wedded wife. To have and to hold, from this day forward, in sickness and in health…"

I'm sure my voice carried across the congregation with bold confidence and crystal clarity. I thought to myself, *this is going very well. I'm glad we're recording the service.* The pastor boomed out the next phrase, "To love and to cherish." With equal flare and volume I declared, "To love and to perish!"

Instantly aware of my *faux pas*, I bellowed, "*Cherish!*"

It was too late; *perish* hung there in space—a word long to be remembered by all.

Sandy smiled. Pastor Cleveland grinned. The congregation snickered. And I, with beet-red face, simply stood there with a renewed sense of personal fallibility.

We made it through the remainder of the ceremony without further incident. But then came the merciless ribbing as family and friends kidded me about the error. At first I thought I should pretend it had been purposeful, a clever act to add some spice to the service. Instead, I humbly owned my mistake and bore the consequences.

Following the reception, we ran through a shower of rice, climbed into our car, and headed for our honeymoon in northern Michigan. Tin cans clanged behind us for several miles.

Our first stop was a fancy motel near Pontiac—$35 for a special room (big money in those days). We stayed one night, then headed to the Upper Peninsula and Sault Saint Marie. Another one-night stay.

The next morning I stopped at a little army surplus store and asked Sandy to wait in the car. Soon I returned with a small pup tent and a few camping supplies. I knew she had never been camping before and I wanted to treat her to a unique experience while on our honeymoon. I figured this would be a fitting prelude to many years of enjoyable camping during our life together.

How I Botched Our Honeymoon

We drove across the border into Canada and began looking for the perfect spot to spend our first night together in the woods.

As we began to scout out a place to set up camp, we couldn't find anything like I had been accustomed to in the Pacific Northwest. The further north we drove, the thicker the undergrowth and the worse the camping conditions. Night drew near. Raindrops appeared on the windshield. I tasted the first spoonful of frustration.

We finally arrived at a campground, only to find every established camping spot taken. However, I was able to locate a patch of grass near the entrance with a small fire ring. We claimed it. I jumped out and hurriedly erected the tent (did I say it was small?). I tossed the double sleeping bag inside and we piled into the tent.

Within a few moments we both discovered something new about my bride—she is claustrophobic. The small tent and cramped bag eventually caused her to flee to the car.

I remained in the tent, determined to see this thing through. Alone and awake, I urged the dawn to arrive so I could get out of the tiny tent and fix breakfast over a fire. The night dragged on.

As soon as the faintest light appeared, I crawled out and rounded up some damp wood to start a fire. Sandy staggered out of the car to observe my camp-cooking skills. I noted she looked different than she did walking down the aisle a few nights before.

With mounting frustration, I tried desperately to coax the wet wood into a flame. A frying pan with gooey pancake batter sat nearby in the drizzling rain. Smoke filled my eyes and lungs. My nose ran. I groused about my city-slicker wife. Finally, in exasperation, I gave up on breakfast and gathered all the camping gear and hurled it into the trunk of the car. I slammed the lid and barked, "Get in the car." We left the scene with tires spraying mud and gravel in every direction.

For at least an hour we traveled in stony silence—two people who had so recently known marital bliss, now mired in the swamp of human discord.

What had begun as a romantic, delightful honeymoon had disintegrated into a tense, angry conflict. Sweet unity fled our marriage.

Eventually, as you might surmise, we resolved the conflict and our happy honeymoon continued. The account of that reconciliation is a story I will keep to myself. Suffice it to say, we enjoyed the process.

The point I want to make here is the senselessness of the conflict and the speediness with which it arose. I blame 99.9 percent of it on myself. I was intolerant, insensitive, inconsiderate, and prideful. I wince as I recall the experience.

Conflict in marriage and in other relationships is often so needless. It is unproductive and, especially to others, unattractive. It undercuts God's will for unity and leaves a bad taste in everyone's mouth.

I heard a sermon on the words of Jesus about being servant-minded. The preacher had a hand towel that he draped across his arm as a symbol of humble service. He referred to it throughout his message.

He said the secret to unity in marriage and other areas of life is to humble ourselves in service to others. Unity is not achieved by lording over another, but by kneeling in service, as Jesus did when he washed his disciple's feet and dried them with a towel.

How I Botched Our Honeymoon

I would like to say that the attitude and behavior I displayed on our first camping excursion was a one-time thing. Sadly, that is not the case. I have had to repent many times and relearn the lesson of the towel. I am blessed to have a forgiving wife.

Though some of my rough edges have smoothed out over the years, the Lord continues to work on those that remain. I marvel at his patience and tenacity. And I am comforted by the promise that he who began a good work in me will keep at it throughout my life.

Chapter 2

The Wyoming Campfire

After our honeymoon, we drove to our first home—a small apartment in the upper-class men's dorm on the campus of a small Midwest Christian College. Sandy was to attend classes and I was to teach in the Philosophy and Religion Department. I don't remember whether she ever sat in one of my courses. If she didn't, that was probably a good thing.

After a few years we heard the call to "Go West, Young Couple, Go West." So we packed up our meager belongings and hooked the U-Haul trailer to the back of our Buick.

After fixing a flat tire somewhere along the way, we continued to Wyoming and the Yellowstone and Grand Teton National Parks. Between these parks, we discovered a narrow slice of national forest…and a dirt road. Since we had camping gear tucked in the trunk, we headed up this little road looking for an idyllic place to spend a few days.

Deeper into the forest we drove on the narrowing road—certainly not the place for a car and trailer. Finally, with night falling, we located an isolated spot on a bank overlooking the headwaters of the Snake River. We made camp, built a fire, and sat near enough to poke the coals with sticks as we reminisced. With the fire nearly out, we entered the tent and crawled into our sleeping bags.

The next morning we bolted upright in unison to the sound of a rifle shot. And then another. Before long we discovered that we were in a prime location for the opening day of hunting season! In fact, within 200 yards of us a hunter brought down a large elk.

All that day we heard shots near and far and watched as off-road vehicles passed by on the little road. Not one person looked our way without a quizzical expression that asked, "How in the world did they get that trailer in here?" and, "Why are they camping here when it's hunting season?"

We stuck it out and as the day continued we noted a decline in gunfire and traffic.

The second night we made another fire. Flames and sparks leaped into the air. I don't recall, but perhaps we roasted a few marshmallows. We sat on a log and watched the burning wood. We had a good pile of fuel, so we kept the fire bright and warm long into the night. We were two bumps on a log encircled by darkness, illuminated by a campfire.

Sometime near midnight we detected an approaching noise out in the blackness. Like startled deer, our senses snapped to attention. I dashed to the tent for my .22 revolver. Closer the noise came, crashing through brush. A wild animal? A wounded grizzly? How could such a little gun protect us from imminent slaughter?

The Wyoming Campfire

Suddenly, a somewhat inebriated man splashed his way across the river and stumbled into camp. He had been hunting up on the mountainside when darkness fell and had lost his way. All he could see was our fire and so he set out cross-country to reach that light. He was wet, bruised, and exhausted.

While he warmed himself, I unhitched the trailer so we could drive him to the camping spot where his buddies were doubtless gathered in concern.

I have wondered what would have happened to that lost person in the forest had we not started a campfire. I have also thought of Jesus' words regarding the beacon effect of a glowing city on top of a hill.

We don't know who's watching us. We don't know who's out there stumbling in the darkness, moving toward our light. We can't see what God sees. But we can keep feeding the fire and making sure that our lives radiate warmth, fellowship, and safety.

Chapter 3

Family Camping
Gone Awry

We went camping as a family in the early 1980s. Our four children ranged in age from a toddler of three to a preteen of 12.

I was the pastor of a church just north of Seattle and when vacation time came along I decided to introduce my family to the wonders of the out-of-doors. After all, my parents took me and my sister for many campouts and I wanted to pass on that legacy to my family.

We had an aging Oldsmobile station wagon and a meager assortment of camping items. When our neighbors found out we were planning to buy a tent, they insisted on loaning us their large canvas tent. They had used it the previous year and said it worked fine.

We collected a supply of cooking gear, sleeping bags, camp stools, and a few boxes of assorted food. I got a fishing license and rustled up a rod and reel. This was going to be a great adventure, one that would launch us into a series of future camping trips and a plethora of pleasant life-time memories.

We stuffed the car and loaded more things on top. Miraculously, we found space for all six of us inside. Everyone was excited as we pulled out of the driveway and headed for the Cascade Mountains.

"Where are we going, Dad?" I told them of this beautiful place a couple of hours away up an old Forest Service road. "It will be great fun for all of us." Sandy seemed unusually quiet.

After passing North Bend on Interstate 90, we turned north and headed up a gravel road that followed the Middle Fork of the Snoqualmie River. Eventually, we came to a place where I had previously lived for a summer as a Forest Service patrolman.

I pointed out where the Camp Brown cabin used to be and explained that the river had flooded and washed the building away. As we continued, the road deteriorated. When we came to the confluence of the Taylor and Middle Fork rivers I thought we might find a nice spot at the Taylor River Campground. No luck; the place had been flooded out and closed as a campground.

"O well," I said, "we'll find a great spot on up the road along the river someplace."

"How much further, Dad?" "When are we going to get there?" "I gotta go potty."

Sandy tried to encourage everyone as best she could, but I noticed that her voice was developing a nervous quality.

Finally, I found what appeared to be a flat piece of ground right next to the river. The rustic spot was down a short hill from the road and I managed to pull off enough so another car could pass if necessary.

The river was moving swiftly and the thought of our toddler going for an unplanned swim caused us to place the two smaller children under the close supervision of the older kids while Mom and I unloaded the car. Up and down the hill we went, moving all of our camping supplies to the flat grassy area.

At this point, I should note the absence of a bathroom, a picnic table, and a fire pit.

The day was winding down and it would be suppertime soon, so we decided to fly into action and erect the tent. Jonathan and I did the honors while Mom rode herd on the others and tried to develop some kind of a cooking/eating area.

We opened the tent bag and discovered the pungent odor of mildew. As we unfolded the damp canvas we realized that the owners had disassembled it in the rain a year earlier and never unpacked the tent later to dry it out. In spite of a few rotten cords that broke easily, we managed to erect the edifice and open the flaps. The inside walls were covered with slimy mold and the whole thing stunk worse than a wet barnyard.

When I announced our findings, Sandy moaned.

We next built a fire pit with river rock and collected enough wood to get a smoky fire going. We heated water and then took hot wet towels into the tent to rub down the sides and reduce the mold and smell.

Darkness fell and we were still working on the moldy tent. During the process we were able to eat some food and swat mosquitoes. Sandy laid out the sleeping bags in the tent and we all turned in for the night. While the tent might have been roomy for four people, it was wall to wall for six sleeping bags.

A long night ensued. Just when silence might permit sleep, the air would be broken with, "I gotta go potty," or "I need a drink of water," or "This place stinks!" or "There's a rock under my bed."

When morning finally came we stumbled out and I hunkered over the fire to fix pancakes. I don't recall how they turned out, but my guess is they lacked the culinary quality of the home-cooked variety.

During the morning it was universally agreed to break camp and head home. This camping trip had turned into a disaster and the sooner we placed it behind us, the better. Maybe next time things would go better. "Don't count on a next time," said Sandy.

We lugged all of the junk back up the hill to the car and made ready to leave. As I rounded the vehicle to get in the driver's side, my heart, soul, and mind sank. The right front tire was flatter than one of the uneaten pancakes I had tossed into the bushes.

Out came everything from the back of the station wagon and I retrieved the "donut" spare and a rusty jack. What followed next is barred permanently from my memory. Suffice it to say, with difficulty I was able to change the tire and turn the car around for the homeward trip.

Much to the great relief of all, we made it home without injury or permanent family discord. I returned the tent to the owners and noted its condition.

As I recall this family campout, I think of several instructive applications. First, the moldy tent. We read in Genesis about Lot pitching his tent toward Sodom and Abram placing his tent near the Oaks of Mamre (Chapter 13). In Exodus and elsewhere we read of the "tent of meeting" where God met his people. The Apostle Paul talked about the earthly tent in which we dwell.

Paul also spoke of the "household of faith" as a spiritual structure or tabernacle and our bodies as temples of the Holy Spirit. Comparing these images with the moldy tent described above causes me to appreciate the importance of caring for the enclosure of my faith. Do I maintain it in good order? Or do I apathetically allow mold to develop and mildew to accumulate?

Another application pertains to our choices and the effects they have on others. Had I considered the ages and interests of my children (not to mention my wife), I would have made better plans and selected a place with appropriate accommodations for my young family. I allowed my own adventurous appetite to rule the occasion.

Third, sometimes a "bowl of cherries" kind of day turns into a pile of pits. Things don't work out like we plan. Moldy problems of the past return to foul our day. The blood-sucking mosquitoes of multiple mistakes irritate us. Smoke gets in our eyes.

But always nearby rolls the river of God's presence. Like the tree by the rivers of water in Psalm 1, we can absorb God's peace and be nourished by his provision.

I don't recall that we ever went tent camping again as a whole family. We did, however, go many times in smaller numbers. I've enjoyed excursions with one or two family members and relish the assorted memories. Maybe that's another point of application. Sometimes we need the camaraderie and fellowship that two or three provide…as well as the opportunity to impact one or two lives with concentrated attention.

Chapter 4

Bonding With Jonathan

When Jonathan turned 12 I bought a 14-foot inflatable boat and an outboard motor. During that summer we began a series of annual adventures that took us throughout Puget Sound, the San Juan Islands, and into the Canadian waters of the Gulf Islands and Desolation Sound.

On one of our earlier trips we found a small isolated island in the San Juans and made preparations to spend the night. It was not possible to pull the Achilles up on the beach, so we found a small cove and tied the bow and the stern to opposite ends of the cove so it wouldn't rub against the rugged rocks.

When we woke the next morning we faced a low tide and a boat swinging in the air. We had to wait for the tide to rise before packing and leaving.

That was the same night that a high tide brought the water within inches of our sleeping bags. We learned some important lessons about reading tide charts more carefully.

During the day we would scoot across the water to check out various points of interest. We found pleasure "jumping" the wakes of power boats that pushed through the waterways.

Quite by accident, we found we could perpetually surf the wake of a fast moving cabin cruiser by angling our inflatable down the wake. By going "downhill" we could throttle back our motor and still keep up with a larger boat.

One hot day the water was perfectly still and we decided to just float aimlessly about. We made a make-shift table between us and played several card games. We luxuriated in the sun and reveled in the surrounding sea. We drank cold Pepsi from a cooler and somewhere along the line we found ourselves exclaiming, "This is livin'!"

We also had our share of "hairy" experiences, like getting caught in a rip tide on a windy day that nearly swamped the boat. Or the time we were surrounded by Orca whales.

Long after we sold the Achilles, we continued to carve out annual adventure trips that took us into Alaska, Prince Rupert, the Queen Charlotte Islands, and the interior of British Columbia. We've fished together, hiked together, explored together, and even hunted elusive chukars together.

During the four or five years we explored the sea, and our subsequent adventures on land, we accumulated many hours of just sitting together on a beach, by a lake, or at some other place of beauty where we read the Bible, prayed, and talked. The bonding that occurred during those shared experiences is one reason we love being together today.

I've thought of Jesus and the times he drew his disciples away from the crowds to be with them in the great out-of-doors.

He seemed attracted to the mountains and hills, as well as the beaches and waters of Lake Galilee. As he shared these places and times with his closest friends, he used the particulars of nature to illustrate kingdom truths.

As I look back on the formative times I spent with Jonathan, I am reminded of my Heavenly Father's desire to spend time with me in all the adventures of life, teaching me about him and using me to bless the lives of others. We are not called to a humdrum life or a rutted existence, but rather to a grand procession of unique experiences that bind us all the more to the great Companion of our souls.

I am also reminded that it takes time to grow a relationship. Whether it's a husband-wife connection, a parent-child link, a friend-to-friend association, or even deepening ties with the Lord, bonding requires the sacrifice of time and the purposeful investment of personal effort.

There is nothing quite as powerful as the bonding power of a shared adventure—whether it be in the wide world of nature, the challenges of daily life, or in the intimacy of prayer.

Chapter 5

Showdown In the Kitchen

In our second year of marriage we purchased a white Spitz puppy. During the day, while we were a mile away at Greenville College where I worked and Sandy took classes, the dog ate, slept, and entertained itself as little puppies do. We kept her penned in a corner of the kitchen with paper on the floor. As she grew, so did her exploratory instincts. Soon she was knocking down the make-shift cage and wandering through the house chewing on things and depositing unmentionable substances.

Schoen (as we called her) was no dummy. She learned tricks quickly and even demonstrated a clear understanding of the never-leave-the-kitchen-on-your-own rule. She would come to the edge of the linoleum and stop for permission before advancing onto the hardwood floor and carpets. As long as we were there, she showed perfect obedience. Nice doggie.

However, as soon as we would leave the house and close the door behind us, Schoen would advance stealthily into the living room to begin her destructive ways. After waiting a moment, I would re-enter the kitchen quickly to catch her in the act. Each time she would cower to the floor and empty her bladder.

Again and again I tried to force my will on her, threatening great wrath should she place one paw on the hardwood floor. Again and again she would wait until she thought we were gone, and then proceed as though she owned the house.

I was determined to teach this head-strong animal to stay in that kitchen while we were gone. Sandy and I would leave, pretending happily to be going for the day, even getting in the car and backing down the driveway…only to quietly open the door and sneak back to the window where we'd wait for the little demon to cross the line. Then I'd roar into the house and scold the errant dog.

Moving my strategy to the next level, I created a trip-wire that was connected to a pole with several pots and pans hanging from the top. The plan was for her to trip the wire as she went into the living room which, in turn, would rain down a noisy squall of cookware. This racket would evoke serious apoplexy and cure the dog once and for all from sneaking out of the kitchen.

The next morning, I set the trap and cheerfully bade Schoen farewell as Sandy and I left the house and drove the car down the driveway. Then we both crept back and took our positions at the window. We waited and watched as the dog walked over to the edge of the kitchen floor.

You could almost see the wheels turning as she contemplated her next move. Then, convinced in her doggie mind that we were indeed gone, she crossed the line and tripped the wire. As the falling pots and pans clanged around her, she dashed wildly through the house, spraying urine in every direction.

What happened next was not pretty. I will say, however, that I did not beat the dog. I did thrash her severely with words and I probably repeated the dreaded phrase, "Bad dog!" several times.

It was about then that I accepted defeat. We fixed a place outside for her in the carport and let her in only when we were there. We also did some rehab on the house to bring it back to its pre-puppy state.

In time, we grew to be exceedingly fond of Schoen. For six years, she lived happily among us. When we moved and could not take her with us, Sandy's parents enjoyed her for another seven years.

Yes, I feel badly as I look back on my impatience. I feel sorry I got so wrapped up in a scheme that was doomed from the outset. I still regret my harsh words and stern disciplinary ways.

My inept dog-training experience continues as a good reminder to me that I can become too focused and too demanding over something that is really not all that important in the big scheme of things. My failure with Schoen was more about me than about her. I created an impossible standard and wouldn't back off.

Wow! What if God treated me like I treated that little dog? I'm so glad for his persistent grace, perpetual patience, unfailing mercy, and steadfast love.

Chapter 6

Our Maniacal Brittany

Our youngest of four children wanted a puppy. We debated the topic for weeks. Finally, I gave in with the provision that we both had to agree on the breed and the specific dog. I wanted a dog that I could take chukar hunting and Julia wanted a companion. We settled on a Brittany spaniel.

Years before, Sandy and I had raised registered Alaskan malamutes and showed them in the ring. We knew the benefits of a good pedigree and so Julia and I began searching for the perfect Brittany. We scoured the classifieds and followed up every lead. Finally, we drove a hundred miles to attend a hunting dog sporting event known as field trials.

After a few inquiries, we located a breeder who had a pregnant Brittany. We made arrangements to acquire one of the pups. It would be a few months, so I gave the owner a down payment. She promised to call us when the pups were a few weeks old so we could come and make our selection. Then it would be another few weeks before we could acquire the dog.

I recall the conversation as the woman interviewed us about our knowledge of dogs and our intentions regarding the Brittany. "You know, these dogs are bred to run. If you want a nice quiet dog to sit at your feet, you need to look elsewhere."

Her counsel went in one ear and out the other. Surely with my dog-training expertise I could condition the dog to be a good pet for Julia and a dandy hunting dog for me.

The weeks dragged by, but finally the big day came. We drove to the kennel, selected a puppy, and headed home. We named our new family member, Paige. We had a fenced yard for the days and we let the dog sleep inside the house at night in a portable kennel.

All went well for a few months. She bounded around the backyard and played tirelessly. When we took her for walks, she strained at the leash to investigate whatever lay ahead. Nice doggie.

We learned early on that we could not let Paige run free because she would take off and never look back. We lived near the beach and would take her down to the water and unclip the leash. She would shoot away from us like a bullet and vanish within seconds. Eventually we would find her, or someone would call us after reading our number on her collar. "We've got your dog," they'd say.

As Paige neared her first birthday, her energy level seemed to soar. She would not, could not, walk alongside us, but continually strained forward with all her might. She would run circles for hours in the backyard. I took her hunting a couple of times and found her amazingly suited for that endeavor.

Our Maniacal Brittany

Sometimes you've got to let a dog go. We all came to that conclusion after cyclone-natured Paige convinced us she could not acquire respect for the property of others. The final straw came at 11:30 p.m. one night when our very angry 16-year-old daughter roused us from sleep with the news that Paige had somehow freed herself from her nighttime kennel. Possessed by doggie demons from the netherworld, she effectively annihilated numerous items. "She's ruined everything!" wailed Julia.

Sandy and I donned our bathrobes and stumbled downstairs to view the carnage. My heart sank. Bad dog! Very bad dog! Bad, bad dog!

Paige had not only ruined most everything in sight, she had gone about it with meticulous precision. For example, she chewed to pieces a set of 24 colored marking pens—each and every one of them. That, of course, explained the color combination on the carpet, furniture, and dog.

Completing her mission in the family room, Paige returned to Julia's room and chewed to smithereens every prized keepsake on the lower shelf of the bookcase, including souvenirs from her trip to Japan. Bad dog! Really, really bad dog!

At that time we had a remodeling project in process and the carpenter took a liking to Paige. When he discovered our decision to find her a new home, he volunteered enthusiastically. "I'm getting married next month and this will be a wonderful wedding present. She loves dogs."

We made the financial arrangements and fully disclosed the dog's wild ways. The day arrived when the bride came to meet her new dog. Amazingly, Paige took to her like a long lost friend. It was like Paige was saying, "Rescue me from this sedate family.

I want to run. O please take me and run with me. I want to be free! I want to be free!"

A few weeks later I asked the carpenter how Paige was doing. He said, "Her leg's in a cast. She was running through the house and somehow got tangled in the lamp cord and broke her leg as she tried to leap free."

The next report about Paige revealed that she had jumped their high fence and mixed her pedigree with a neighborhood scamp.

Dogs can teach us many things. One of the lessons we learned from Paige is that you can't always teach new dogs old tricks. Despite our patient, consistent efforts to train her to heel, she could not comply. She was wired to run and nothing we tried could alter that predisposition.

Likewise, some people seem unable to change. Their personalities are fixed. They appear to be consistently and unalterably set in their negative ways. We regard them as hopeless. But then the Master stretches out his hand and touches the leper. He heals the demoniac and raises Lazarus from the dead. He takes men and women who are bound by sin and releases them to become loving and godly people. He breathes new life into our souls and delivers us from despair and gives us the strength to overcome destructive habits and hurtful attitudes.

Jesus does not give up on us and sell us to another owner. He purchased us for time and eternity and he changes us from one degree to another into his image. No leash is needed as we walk in companionship with him. He is our provider, our guide, our friend. We run only to do his will.

Chapter 7

Dog Shows and Similarities

Before our first child, and during the few years I worked on a graduate degree at Central Washington State University, Sandy and I connected with the Alaskan malamute community. We established Polarpaw Kennel and acquired a few well-papered malamutes.

We started going to dog shows where I would prance one of our dogs around the ring. Occasionally we won a ribbon or trophy. Our kennel name and dogs began to be noticed.

Some owners hired professional handlers to show their dogs. Others, like me, did the honors. At a signal from the ringmaster, I'd enter and run my dog around in a circle in front of the judge(s). Posture, gait, alertness—these and other qualities received scrutiny. Then I'd set the dog in show stance and the judge would check out the animal for blemishes, healthy teeth, and other features.

After my turn I'd exit and the next malamute/handler would enter the ring. This continued until each dog of the breed had its chance. The judge might then ask one or more of us to run our dogs around again. He or she would study the dogs intently to narrow down the decision. Finally, the judge would point to the winner and someone would present the ribbon.

At the end of the show, one dog would be singled out as "Best of Show" and the owner would receive a trophy. I got one of these once (for the dog, not me).

The dog shows we attended were not televised or covered by the national media. These were relatively small gatherings of a local or regional variety and, at least for us, always occurred in the eastern part of Washington State.

We had two show-quality dogs—our male, Shane, and a female called Sno-Star. The latter dog went on to become an international champion after we sold her to a breeder in Wisconsin.

Our short-lived fling into this highly competitive and sometimes vicious world enlarged our understanding of dogs and their owners. For one thing, we learned that *prima donna* dogs don't always act nicely. Before the show—and sometimes during the competition—there would be flare-ups caused by aggressive temperaments. And it wasn't always the larger dogs. Little fluffy fur-balls could be pretty feisty and stir things up, setting other dogs on edge.

We also discovered firsthand the remarkable similarities between dogs and owners. This was true regarding appearance and general demeanor. For example, a rotund madam would either have a Saint Bernard or a smallish Pomeranian—one reflecting her physique or the other bearing witness to her aspirations.

Dog Shows and Similarities

We noted unmistakable connections between puffy-haired women and their puffy little poodles. A long lanky man might have a leggy short-haired hunting dog. And a shaggy-haired master might be seen trotting a sheep dog around the ring. Come to think of it, the Alaskan malamute represents my inclinations better than a dachshund.

My studied opinion is that the person chose the dog because that dog bore a physical trait either like the owner or a trait that the owner wanted to reflect. A large person with a tiny dog may reflect a desire to be smaller…or it might simply be a matter of the person trying to balance out the size issue by presenting two opposites.

In any case, I would suggest to you that subtle forces are at work in our choices of companionship. Just as "birds of a feather flock together," so do we tend to gravitate toward those who share similar opinions, interests, and even physical characteristics. These associations reinforce our own ideas, preferences, and behavior.

That's why it's good to foster friendships with "different" people. For our own well-rounded benefit, we need to get out of our comfort zones and hobnob with those who come from different backgrounds and who may have "foreign" perspectives. We who love God should find our common denominator in him, rather than in those who agree with our preferences, dress codes, or eating practices.

Chapter 8

Chasing Chukars

I have never killed a deer or elk or bear or any other game animal. Nor do I have a rifle to accomplish such deeds. I have good friends who are avid hunters and I have no problem cheering them on. But as for me, I'll stick with beef.

On the other hand, I love to hunt pheasant, grouse, and quail. I have a shotgun for this purpose. Once I even had a hunting dog who took to bird hunting like a sled dog takes to a harness.

By far, my favorite game bird is the chukar. There's a simple reason for this: Chukars are difficult to find and even harder to bring down. They are elusive and they live in difficult terrain. They thrive in dry areas with steep rock outcroppings and minimal foliage. Chukars get their name from the chuk-chuk-chuka-chuka sounds they make.

I have no compunctions hunting chukars because they seem to have all the advantages. And just maybe they enjoy outwitting those who doggedly pursue them. I know there are those who look with disdain upon a hunter of animals or birds. Yet, I cannot imagine anyone objecting to a person going after chukars. This is because the chances of the hunter actually getting a chukar is so miniscule as to border on the impossible.

Over the years I've philosophized about chukars and their evasive skills. I am coming to the conclusion that these feathered creatures were created by God to serve as celestial entertainment. I am not suggesting, mind you, that the birds themselves provide heavenly laughter. Rather, the humor is related to the antics of the hunter as he or she displays a chaotic combination of failure, frustration, and unseemly determination. I am sure I have provided angels with more than a few laughs in my many futile efforts to bring home a chukar for dinner.

Speaking of food, some Bible scholars believe that it was chukar, not quail, that fed the children of Israel during their wilderness wanderings. If that is true, then the miracle is all the more impressive. Did the birds just walk into a frying pan, or did the Israelites have to chase them down?

Chukars are larger than quail, but smaller than sage hen or grouse. They measure about 14 inches long and are part of the partridge family. One source indicates that they have a "light brown back, grey breast, and a buff belly. They have rufous-streaked flanks, red legs, and coral red bills." Actually, they are quite attractive, as you will see if you ever get close enough for a good look.

Chukars originated in the Middle East and today they can be found in many places throughout the world. To this I say, "Well duh!" Hunters can't shoot enough of them to keep the prolific birds from spreading!

Chasing Chukars

Chukars are tasty. My practice is to garner the breast meat, cut it into little cubes, douse the meat in egg batter, roll the cubes in pancake flour, and fry them in bacon fat. Mmmmm. Sometimes I wonder if the delicious sensation of chukar meat is less related to the bird itself and based more on the crafty and herculean effort to obtain the meat in the first place.

I learned about chukars during the four years we lived in Ellensburg, Washington. Located in the central part of the state, the broad valley area is surrounded by hills of sagebrush and some deep canyon terrain. One of these canyons follows the Yakima River southward through rugged and desolate country. Primarily, it was the Yakima Canyon that became for me, chukar paradise.

On a typical outing, a friend and I would drive up to an area high above the river where the top of the canyon wall provided a mesa-type setting for the birds. They tended to reside in this flat and open area dotted with sagebrush and other dry-climate vegetation. They would often congregate near the rim of an outcropping of volcanic rock.

This high perch provided them with an easy escape route. If a coyote came near, they'd simply shove off and fly straight down toward the river. Sometimes they'd stop midway, count noses, and then begin working their way back up the canyon wall.

Okay, so here we are creeping along the open area on top, listening for the telltale chukar sound. We watch for movement among the sagebrush.

Suddenly, we are startled by a roar of flapping wings similar to the sound of 500 747s taking off together. The chukars rise just enough to clear the ground, point their beaks toward the river, and dive-bomb straight down. In the split second available, you bring your shotgun to your shoulder and aim and shoot at the same time, hoping you hit at least one of the fleeing fowl.

With jaw set and adrenalin coursing through your body, you head down the steep slope with shotgun at the ready. You know that the elusive creatures have landed part way down and may wait for you to get near enough for another shot. But just as you come within range, up they rise and down they go. This time they swing to the right or left and disappear from view. You know they are down there so you keep descending, angling toward their last known location. Mounting frustration and vengeance fuel the effort to proceed.

Then, when you reach the place you think they may be, you hear a chuk-chuk-chuka-chuka sound off to the side and above you. That's because the sadistic birds are hot-footing it up the hill. And so begins the down-up-down-up life of the chukar hunter.

Eventually, you find yourself sitting on a rock gasping for air and cursing (in a nice way) the elusive birds. You ask yourself, "Why am I out here chasing these deplorable fowl over this forsaken terrain? What's wrong with me?"

Sometimes I'd bring one of my Alaskan malamutes along. I'd fill his doggy pack with a thermos of coffee, a few granola bars, and a dry shirt or two. Shane eventually got the idea that when I shot the gun on the mesa one of the fleeing birds might fall to the ground. He would race to the area and find or run down a wounded bird. Then he'd snag the chukar in his mouth and shake it while I ran toward him yelling, "No Shane, no! Don't eat it!"

Chasing Chukars

After four years, we moved to Indiana where the term "chukar" never reached my ears. It was part of my past and I tried to put the frustrating hunting episodes out of my mind.

Ten years went by and we moved back to the Northwest where I pastored a church just north of Seattle. Before long, I began thinking about my bird-hunting past and the possibilities of driving the hundred miles to Ellensburg to see what had become of the chukar population.

When the season opened for upland game birds, I shared my enthusiasm with a few friends and suggested that we pile into my van the next morning and head east. Both of these guys had been around the mountain a few times and knew a thing or two about hunting grouse and pheasants; but neither of them had even heard the word, "chukar."

When we arrived, I drove them to a high sagebrush mesa where we stopped to reconnoiter. I told them what to listen for and what to expect when the covey of chukars rose to flee. We spread out and walked across the mesa with shotguns at the ready.

By late morning we had seen nothing. I began to discern a tone of disbelief. They suggested that I was staging this whole thing just to get out of Seattle and enjoy the out-of-doors. The more they talked, the more they established the conviction that the whole trip was something akin to a practical joke. They even openly accused me of making up the term, "chukar."

Noon arrived and we decided to drive into town for lunch. The waitress brought the menus and one of my friends said, "Pardon me, but may I ask you a question? Are there any chukars around here?" She responded, "What's a chukar?"

That was not helpful. Again I was pressed into a defensive mode and sought more earnestly to convince them that chukars were real and worth pursuing.

Reactivating my enthusiasm, I said, "Hey, I know another place where we might find some chukars. Let's go check it out." They followed me out to the van, mumbling something beyond my hearing.

As we drove along slowly atop a broad mesa, scanning the area for chukars, a dozen or so ran across the dirt road in front of us. I quietly stopped, got out with my shotgun and slowly walked toward the area where the birds were chukaring away. Discerning my presence, they suddenly rose and headed away from me, but not before I got off two shots.

I raced to the place and found a chukar on the ground. As I carried it to the vehicle, I saw my two friends standing by the back of the van with matching expressions of consternation. Their guns were in the back of the van and they couldn't open the locked lid. I was so intent on going after the chukars that I completely forgot to wait for them to retrieve their shotguns.

The good part of the episode was the proof I held in my hand. No more could they deny the existence of chukars. No more could they ridicule me about making up a story concerning these upland game birds. Instead, they now had a tale to tell of the pastor who locked their guns in the trunk while he went after the game by himself.

And then there was the time I was out hunting chukars with my Malamute and he attacked a porcupine. Or the time a friend, who didn't want to shoot birds, came along as a sort of human bird dog to scare up hiding chukars, sage hens, Hungarian partridges, or any other game bird in the vicinity. Or the time I took my Brittany spaniel along and worked her so hard I had to lift her up and place her in the back of the pickup for the ride home.

It's been 20 years now since I've chased chukars and I wonder whether I will ever get out the old shotgun again. I'm afraid those days are gone. Now is the time for remembrance…and thanksgiving that no ill befell me during those treks through sagebrush and along the steep rocky hillsides. Now is the time in life to enjoy those ready-to-eat roasted chickens from the grocery store and pretend they are chukars.

Chapter 9

Landcruising In the Land Cruiser

The Toyota Motor Company came to the United States in 1957 and the Land Cruiser was introduced in 1958. One vehicle was sold that year. However, by the early 1960s the Land Cruiser had become the number one vehicle sold by Toyota in the United States and opened the way for their phenomenal success with passenger cars. It was truly a flagship vehicle for Toyota, not only in the U.S., but in other countries as well.

My experience with the Toyota Land Cruiser (TLC) began in 1969 when I bought an early '60s model. I kept it for two years and ran it hard through the sagebrush country of Eastern Washington and up the foothills of the Cascade Mountains.

A few of our TLC adventures will give you an idea of the place this vehicle has played in our lives. One time, Sandy and I drove the Land Cruiser over Stevens Pass to Everett, Washington where I was scheduled to preach at a church. Always the entrepreneur, I rigged up a platform bed in the back of the vehicle. We found a quiet side-street and crawled into the back to sleep.

Never mind that it was raining outside and that we were unable to open the windows, and that our breathing fogged the windows and created drops of moisture on the roof above us. And never mind that we couldn't stand or move around, or that our Sunday clothes were hanging on a hook wrinkling in the soggy air.

The sleepless night finally ended and we set about to dress in the cramped quarters. We then drove to a gas station where we used the restrooms to brush our teeth and comb our hair. I think I shaved with cold water. It was not the best way to prepare oneself to stand in the pulpit and preach the Gospel.

In Ellensburg we lived near a mountain where an unimproved "road" switch-backed its way up the side. We liked to drive up that narrow dirt road to gain a view of the valley and to give our TLC a workout.

One evening in late fall, a couple joined us for dinner at our small rented house. I said, "Hey, let's take a ride up the hill and see the lights of Ellensburg." So we piled in the Land Cruiser and drove the half mile to the foot of the mountain.

The nights were chilly at this time of year and the muddy roads would harden for easy passage in the morning. However, during the day, the sun would warm the earth and the top layer of dirt would turn to mud...a fact I failed to incorporate into my thinking. I just assumed it was cold enough for the road to be hard.

Unfortunately, about a third of the way up the hill, I realized that the tires—already in four-wheel drive—were churning. Our forward progress ceased and we began to slide sideways toward the edge of the road and a steep drop-off to the floor of the valley. There was not a single thing I could do but brace myself for multiple rollovers down the hill. I yelled, "Hang on, we're going down!" Then, miraculously, the vehicle stopped sliding and we were able to gingerly extricate ourselves from the vehicle and onto the muddy ground.

We left the Land Cruiser and started to slip-slide our way down the road on foot. By the time we reached pavement, our shoes and socks were gooey with mud. The next morning the ground was frozen and I was able to retrieve the Land Cruiser without incident.

Another time I was hill-climbing with the Land Cruiser in a canyon where tracks indicated others had gone up the steep slope. I thought, *if someone else has done this, so can I.* I put the rig in four-wheel drive and began my ascent. I made it more than half way when the angle of the climb, the looseness of the soil, and my worn tire treads converged to stop my progress. I had power, but no traction to proceed.

As I began sliding backwards, I jammed the gearshift into reverse and let out the clutch to take advantage of the compression and to help me control the descent. Straining my neck, I looked over my right shoulder and tried to maneuver around trees and other obstacles on the downward trip. It was a sobering experience, not only for me but also for my terrified passenger.

When Sandy was nine-months pregnant with our first child, I shoehorned her into the Land Cruiser and we went off in search of bumpy ground to stimulate labor. No luck. A few days later she checked into the hospital and labor was properly induced.

I recall fording streams with that first Land Cruiser and also using it to haul our dogs around. It was a fun machine and I hated to part with it when we moved from Ellensburg to Winona Lake, Indiana.

The common denominator in my memories of this early TLC seems to be the issue of traction. I learned that you can have the greatest off-road vehicle known to man and still be unable to make your destination because of poor tires. You've got to have deep treads and be willing to chain up when the ground turns to ice. Even when plowing through water you must be able to grip the rocky streambed.

Traction is vital to our spiritual lives as well. When our tires of faith become bald and we slide dangerously in the rain of discouragement or on the ice of hardship, it is time to get serious about our spiritual safety and fix the problem. We need tires with tread, tires that will grip the road and carry us to our destination.

When we drive through the waters of woe, we need traction. When we encounter the slimy clay of temptation, we need traction. When we come upon the snow-covered roadway of a cold heart, we need traction. When the mud of self-pity is deep and our tires of faith begin to spin, we need traction. When the hill of trial is steep before us, we need traction. To get through this life and reach heaven's gate, we need traction.

At times, like Peter's denial, we may have a blowout along the way. Or over time we may allow a slow leak of neglect to impede our progress. When our spiritual vitality and focus becomes flat, we need to call for Roadside Assistance to fix the problem. God will repair our heart and pump fresh life into our souls and steer us forward toward his purposes and pleasure.

Landcruising In the Land Cruiser

We can have all the power of heaven under the hood and a tank full of premium fuel, but unless we apply that power to the road, we will remain at the curb of stagnation. We need tires of application. Tires with tread. Tires that grip the road. We need axels of trust and obedience, and the four deep-treaded tires of worship, witness, faithfulness, and service.

Take time today to check your tires for traction. Make sure you're ready for the variety of road conditions that lie ahead.

Chapter 10

Stranded On the Ferry

I bought a new Toyota Land Cruiser in 1995 and obtained a specialized license plate that reads, "LNDCRUZN." I had always wanted a vehicle I could "trick out" for off-road exploration and after considerable research, I opted for the TLC. During the next several months I ordered specialty parts from U.S. locations and Australia. Here is a partial list of the 30-plus modifications and additions:

- 9,000-pound Warn Winch and Custom Brush Guard
- Heavy Duty Metal Box Over Winch
- BF Goodrich 285x16R7.5 Mud Tires
- ARB Air Lockers, Front and Back
- Front and Rear Heavy-Duty Progressive Coil Springs
- Kaymar Back Bumper, Tire and Gas Carriers (Australia)
- Roller Drawer System (Australia)
- Dual Battery System With Isolator
- Filtered Breather Tubs (Front/Rear Diffs, Gear Box/ Transfer Case)
- Two KC 6-inch 150 Amp Front Lights

- Air Compressor and Tank With Outside Connector
- ARB Roof Rack (Australia)

Okay, you get the picture. The Land Cruiser was equipped for heavy-duty off-roading. I tell you this because I want to establish an image in your mind for what I am now about to relate.

As I mentioned in chapter four, from the time my son was about 12 years old we embarked on an annual father-son adventure. Some of these were boating trips, some were camping odysseys (like a trip to Alaska), some were guided fishing adventures, and several could be called TLC expeditions.

Right now I'm thinking of a TLC trip that took us to the Queen Charlotte Islands, eight hours by ferry west of Prince Rupert in British Columbia. More specifically, I'm thinking of the painfully embarrassing experience we shared on the way to Prince Rupert.

With the TLC packed with gear (including the roof rack) and the dark green finish polished like a mirror, we boarded a ferry for Victoria on Vancouver Island. From there we drove northward 310 miles to the quaint town of Port Hardy. There we boarded a B.C. Ferry for the 15-hour trip up the Inside Passage to Prince Rupert.

Because we arrived in Port Hardy the night before, we were first in line to board the ferry the next morning. We were directed to a place at the front of the car deck just left of the exit opening. This ferry had giant doors at both ends so the cars would be protected during foul weather.

We got out and stood by the TLC to watch the ferry load, noting with some degree of satisfaction the eyes that fell upon our bright and shiny expedition vehicle. Some people were curious to the point of walking over to get a closer look.

The trip went without incident—except for a game of Scrabble on the passenger deck that I roundly lost to Jonathan. When we approached Prince Rupert, the loud speakers directed all vehicle drivers and passengers to return to the car deck. We moved confidently to the TLC, taking note of those who were showing special interest in our go-anywhere machine.

Finally, the great moment arrived and the giant doors parted in front of us. With a flourish, the attendant pointed to us as the first vehicle to disembark. I responded to his signal by turning the starter key. Nothing happened!

We were dead in the water, so to speak. The engine would not turn over and after a few more signals from the obviously perturbed attendant, the other drivers were directed to navigate around us to exit the ferry. Meanwhile, we busied ourselves troubleshooting the problem. The impressive expedition vehicle sat motionless while cars drove by with gawking people noting our predicament. We could almost hear the mocking conversations and the unrestrained giggles.

When we were the only remaining vehicle on the ferry, the attendant told us a call had been placed for a tow truck to come and take us off the ferry. Mercifully, my resourceful son discovered a blown starter fuse under the hood and quickly replaced it. The engine jumped to life and we rolled off the boat just in time to pass the approaching tow truck.

Since the ferry to the Queen Charlottes didn't leave until the next morning, we had sufficient time to find the cause of the blown fuse. Consequently, we had no problem boarding the ferry for the next leg of our journey. Some of those who had been on the earlier vessel from Port Hardy were also going with us on this ferry. We observed more than a few smiles as folks saw our previously crippled expedition vehicle. I'm sure they wondered whether we would make it off the boat this time.

Appearances can be deceiving. Just like a customized off-road machine, we can appear to others as confident, competent, and courageous—when inside there is something drastically wrong. We can look the part, but lack the power to perform.

In the vessel called the church, we are traveling from the place of birth to another Port. Some "believers" may seem sturdy and shiny and ready for anything. But in reality they are imposters, expedition-looking "saints" who are all show and no substance.

When the time comes to open the doors to heaven, the faulty vehicles will find themselves stranded without a spark of life. A tow truck will come and take them off to the Judgment Seat of Christ…and to the bottomless pit beyond. Blessed are those who troubleshoot and fix their hearts before it's too late!

Chapter 11

Mozart and
Snapping Bungees ℰ᠆

The Queen Charlotte Islands are an archipelago in northern British Columbia. They stretch for 175 miles and consist of two main islands—Graham in the north and Moresby in the south—along with some 150 smaller islands. They are in the "middle of nowhere."

After hearing about these islands, I thought, *this seems like a good place for a father-son adventure.* Jonathan agreed and soon we were making preparations for a 10-day expedition. This included reading books and consulting maps and surfing the Internet. At one point, I found an interesting section in a book that described an isolated place on the west side of one of the Islands that brought us fairly close to the Pacific Ocean. The map showed a finger-like inlet where we could camp and launch our inflatable kayak. We noted that a nearby inlet was dubbed, "The wettest spot on earth."

As mentioned earlier, we packed the Land Cruiser to the gills and made ferry reservations. Once on Vancouver Island, we drove to Port Hardy to catch another ferry to Prince Rupert. From there we took a third vessel to the Queen Charlottes.

Leaving the ferry, we followed the directions in the book to the area where we would depart the Island "highway" and go off-road. One problem: we couldn't locate the Jeep trail.

Back and forth we drove on the main road peering down into the ditch and into the brush for some kind of opening. Then, just when we were ready to throw in the towel, we spied the faint semblance of a passage where we might be able to descend down a patch of gravel and perhaps penetrate the heavy foliage to the west.

Gingerly, the Land Cruiser crept down the embankment and poked its nose into the brush. Then we saw it—the "road"! Thus we began a three to four hour motorized pilgrimage through forsaken land where no other vehicle had gone in the recent past. We crawled up and over and around obstacles, such as fallen trees, rocks, ruts, and roots. We encountered several steep hills and a wide stream. Oh yes, it was also raining.

At times, one of us would walk in front of the vehicle with a large pair of limb loppers to clear away some of the bigger maple saplings that obscured our path. It soon became painfully apparent that the scratches we were incurring on both sides of the Land Cruiser would require the expert buffing of an auto detailer upon our return.

Eventually, we arrived at a small meadow and a modest peninsula of land that jutted into the salt water and provided a pleasant place for our camp. The rain continued unabated.

We set about to erect our wilderness home, including rocks for the fire pit and an amazing array of tarps to cover the area and keep us dry. Fortunately, there were enough trees nearby to make our canopy possible.

Now when I say "amazing array" I am understating the scene. We used at least five tarps, with two of them in the 12 x 18 foot category. I always carry a bag of 40 or so multi-colored bungee cords, and we employed every one of them plus strands of rope and twine. We used poles to hold up any sagging sections and we even dug ditches to carry away the runoff from the tarps. We erected our tent under the tarps for extra protection. When we finished we christened our creation, "Bungee City."

By then it was getting late and we crawled into our bags for the night. We fell asleep listening to the gentle pattering of rain on our expansive tarp roof.

The next morning we scoured the area for dry wood. Finding none, we collected bits and pieces of wet fuel that can be best described as waterlogged. These we piled on a wad of paper in our fire pit and doused them with a cup of white gas. Whoosh! For a few seconds we had a nice blaze. Undaunted, we took a small piece of dry wood from inside the vehicle and scrapped off a pile of wood shavings and surrounded them with small sticks of wet wood, followed by bigger pieces. I was sure my Boy Scout training would do the trick.

The dry wood leaped to life as the flame of the match made contact, but soon we were gazing at a diminishing column of smoke. Now things got serious. I went to the Land Cruiser and extracted a highway flare and started it, thrusting it into the still smoking wood. "This will do it," I said.

But it didn't. In fact, every single thing we tried failed to ignite a sustainable fire. We finally yielded to failure and put the axe and matches away. The rain continued.

Giving in to the downpour, we decided to inflate our sea kayak and prepare to navigate the finger of water to the Pacific Ocean.

As we paddled away from Bungee City we noted a weakness in our calculations. Instead of riding with an outgoing tide, we were fighting against the current. Too eager to see what was ahead, we paddled our way through the rain. After a few hundred yards we found a small bay where we could find some relief from the stronger current of the channel. We debarked and explored.

When we came back to the kayak, we discovered that the tide was changing and now we were faced with either floating down toward the ocean or fighting our way back to our camp. Noting the deterioration of the weather and the lateness of the hour, we decided we had better get back to home base while we could.

It was a good thing we turned around because the rain transitioned into a squall and the wind became a gale. We sat in our camp chairs under the tarp and watched the mounting storm…and wondered what lie ahead.

The first thing to go was one of the weaker bungees. It snapped and swished through the air like a speeding bullet. Then another bungee broke and another. One after another, the bungees snapped and we watched the roof disintegrate before us. The tent was ripped from the ground and the pole frame broke.

What did we do? We turned the Land Cruiser around so the tailgate was away from the wind and we got out our little stove and brewed a cup of Starbucks coffee. We retrieved a package of cookies and put a Mozart CD in the player. And then, with bungees zinging through the air and tarps flapping wildly about, and our tent destroyed beyond use, we huddled together and sipped our brew. And one of us said, "Now this is livin'!"

In the midst of this hurricane-like storm, we both seemed to think the same thing at the same time: That stream we forded to get here will be running high. And what about those steep sections of road and the possibility of mudslides? We rose together, tossed out the remains of the coffee and got busy deflating and storing the kayak and stuffing every bit of equipment into the Land Cruiser for a hasty retreat.

The stream was indeed running full and water came over the floorboards. And there were loose rocks and mud to deal with. But we made it back to the main island road and began looking for a safe place to regroup and prepare for the long trip home.

Several points of application come to mind, but let me explore this one—the water-logged wood. I have never been in a situation where I could not start a fire given the tools we had at that spot in the Queen Charlotte Islands. I tried every trick I could think of without success. That wood was simply incapable of providing heat.

I have met people like that who claim to be Christian, yet lack "burnability." They are water-logged in either legalism or apathy. They have the form of godliness, but deny the power. They are unmoved by powerful sermons and uninspired by compelling truth. They lie about on the spiritual landscape soaking in the drippings of a godless culture. They cannot generate the prayer of Amy Carmichael, "Make me thy fuel, flame of God."

To the sogginess of declining spirituality, we can add the destructive force of hellish winds—gales of adversity, hurricanes of tragedy, cyclones of calamity—that snap the cords of earthly attachment and shred the tarps of worldly protection. Life falls apart.

Jesus said those who hear and do his Word will be like the man who builds his house on the rock. The winds will come and the floods will beat upon that house, but it will stand firm in the storm.

Chapter 12

The Rooftop Tent ❧

During the time I was outfitting my Land Cruiser for off-road use, I read about a company that sold rooftop tents. The price was high and I would need to replace my roof rack with a larger one. So I decided to design my own.

The tent is roomy for one person, but crowded for two. Sandy and I tried it out in the backyard and found it mildly uncomfortable. (Kind of funny now that I think about it—two adults camping in the backyard.)

Later, Jonathan and I slept in the tent off-road during a chukar-hunting trip in Eastern Washington. To say it was a miserable experience fails to adequately describe the occasion. Not only was it too crowded, we spent the night fearing that our combined weight would drop us through the vehicle roof at any moment.

After that, the tent was a solo deal and I was the only one to use it. One time I followed an old dozer road up the side of a mountain. I probably shouldn't have been there but I wanted to see how far I could get. When the "road" became a hiking trail, I found a semi-level spot and erected the rooftop tent. I was sure no one was anywhere near me.

The next morning, while I was still in my sleeping bag, I heard voices and chuckles. I peeked out and saw three hikers heading up the trail. They were shaking their heads as they moved away.

One summer I made plans to go with a friend on a kayak trip through the Broken Islands on the west coast of Vancouver Island. It was during the week Sandy was to be in Michigan visiting her mother. As the kayak trip drew near, my friend from California had to cancel. I was left alone with nothing to do.

I decided to take the Land Cruiser into Canada to explore back roads and to spend my nights in the rooftop tent. I drove eastward out of Vancouver on Highway 1 until I hit Highway 3 at Hope, B.C. Then I headed southeasterly through E.C. Manning Provincial Park. Somewhere along the way I found a dirt road leading into the trees and took it.

Mile after mile I drove deeper into the wilderness until I was unsure if I was actually on a road. Finally, 20 miles or more from the nearest town, I came into a clearing and drove cross-country to an elevated spot where I could look out over the little valley.

I put the platform on the roof rack and erected the tent. Then, as I was preparing supper, I heard the distant sound of thunder. I began to entertain the possibilities of weathering a rip-snorting electrical storm on the top of the Land Cruiser in this exposed place. I also thought of the conversation I had with a couple of forest workers a few miles earlier who said a grizzly bear had been spotted in the area.

Then a flash of lightning streaked across the sky and I made the immediate decision to fold camp and vamoose. I hurriedly dismantled and stored the tent, as well as other bits and pieces of gear. I got in, turned around, and tried to retrace my tracks out of the area. The descending darkness and pelting rain slowed my progress.

When I hit the main dirt road I scooted along until I was out of the woods and back on Highway 3. I located a little town and checked into a motel. The storm raged throughout the night and was so violent it knocked out the electricity and caused flooding in the streets.

I still wonder what would have happened had I stayed in the tent on that isolated hillside deep in the Canadian wilderness.

As I review this off-road adventure to locate a spiritual application, I think of Lot who "pitched his tent toward Sodom" and the poor choice this decision turned out to be.

I also think of drawing a parallel with the Old Testament "tent of meeting" that travelled with the children of Israel from place to place. Perhaps I should write of God's presence in the midst of our wanderings.

Or maybe I should try to tie my experience into the tent-making talents of the Apostle Paul and how he used this trade to support himself and others.

However, the more I think about it, the more I keep bumping into the line, "You gotta know when to fold." I also think of a related bit of advice about knowing when to fight, when to go with the flow, and when to flee.

Some of us who have a few extra risk-taking genes can easily get into trouble by pushing things to the limit and beyond.

Maybe it's a matter of pride or stupidity—or both—that causes us to do things contrary to common sense.

I once heard a sermon about learning to say "no." The preacher didn't focus on evil involvements, but on legitimate things that can absorb our lives to the point where we don't have time for the things God is calling us to do. For one reason or another, we allow ourselves to become overcommitted to the detriment of family and our own health and spiritual growth. We gotta know when to fold our tent and move to safer ground.

Chapter 13

Off-Roading With Sandy

After acquiring my Toyota Land Cruiser in 1995 and adding the bells and whistles for off-road use, I suggested to my wife that we go into the hills and try it out. Years before we had a beat-up Land Cruiser and on various occasions Sandy accompanied me on roaming trips through the sagebrush country of Central Washington. However, those experiences failed to prepare us for one of the early trips we took in the new Land Cruiser.

We drove from Seattle across Snoqualmie Pass to the town of Cle Elum and then headed south into the mountains on a dirt road. I had a vague idea of our destination—Quartz Mountain, a 4,640-foot rounded peak with a commanding view of Mt. Rainier.

The roads getting there were fine and the TLC performed wonderfully. Arriving safely, Sandy and I got out, surveyed the scenery, and inhaled the exhilarating air. How wonderful to be in the wilds with our expedition-equipped vehicle. We had lunch and soaked up the beauty. It would have been absolutely perfect had we then turned around and headed home.

At the top of Quartz we discovered a Jeep trail heading down the opposite side of the mountain. Such trails are rated for difficulty and, as I recall, the sign at the trail opening used the term, "extreme." Hmmm.

I spread out the map and tried to pinpoint our position. GPS technology was relatively new for civilians, and I used mine along with the map. It appeared that this particular Jeep road would eventually lead to Highway 410 which would then permit us to return home through Mt. Rainier National Park. It looked to be a pretty long drive, but we had all afternoon ahead of us.

I suggested we give it a try with the thought that we could always turn around and come back if it got too tough. Even though Sandy said she was game, I detected a slight reticence.

The first thing I noticed as we proceeded down the "trail" was the narrowness. Jeeps are somewhat smaller than Land Cruisers and this permits them to pass through crowded trees relatively easily. The trail seemed to close in on us and though we felt the slaps and scrapes of encroaching foliage, we pressed on.

The second thing I discovered was the absence of turnouts. If we met a vehicle coming the other direction, one of us would have to back up. If I wanted to turn around I'd have to get out and use a chain saw to clear the space.

The third finding was the worsening condition of the road. We encountered deep ruts that required careful straddling and boulders that had to be negotiated. My sense of adventure began to dwindle as I considered the effects of this trip on my shiny TLC.

Finally, we noted the increasing steepness of the trail. We came to one place where it looked really bad and so we stopped to consider the best route down the "chute." I hiked down 50 yards and looked up and pondered the situation for a good 15 minutes. Turning around was an uncomfortable option and I thought, *this is probably the worse stretch. How much worse can it get?* So I let out some of the air in each tire to flatten the tread for better traction and put the vehicle in the lowest gear and we began to inch down the boulder-strewn terrain.

We slid a few times because of sand and rolled off a rock, smashing the left running board. Once we started down there was no possible way to back up, and I was just as certain we would not be able to return this way. This stretch of extreme four-wheeling road was committing us to keep going whether we wanted to or not.

What was Sandy doing during this time? Well, I was impressed with what she was *not* doing. She didn't scream, or jump out and refuse to ride anymore, or even carp at me for putting her and the TLC through this hellish ride. She didn't want to do or say anything to distract me in the least. Later in describing the experience, she used the term "terror."

We both breathed deeply when we completed this stretch and even stopped to get out and look back up the hill. Then we walked around the TLC and checked for damage. Besides the running board and the multiple brush scratches, it appeared to be in one piece. We continued on our way.

Traveling a relatively flat stretch, we came to a fork in the road. There were no signs and both directions seemed reasonable. I had no idea which way to go. Again I got out the map and used the GPS to locate our position. It didn't help much and so, unlike Robert Frost, we took the road that seemed *most* traveled.

We started to climb again and after a half hour we came out onto a clearing that looked over a deep valley. The road down appeared steep, but not as bad as the previous one. We had not passed another vehicle or seen anyone since leaving Cle Elum and we both found ourselves contemplating the long walk out of there should we run out of gas, crash the TLC, or should the road ahead be washed out.

As we stood there looking down into the valley and wondering where this was all going to end, we heard the faint sound of engines. Peering into the valley floor we saw a string of Jeeps heading our direction. The rumbling sounds increased until one vehicle popped out on top and then another one. Seven in all cleared the "summit" and parked in a sort of semi-circle around the TLC.

The guys piled out with obvious interest in how we happened to be there. With beer cans in hand, the tattooed rowdies crowded around us. I thought of my revolver in the vehicle and how useless it was to me just then. I thought of Sandy and how she must be feeling.

But our fears were unfounded and the jolly band took us in as some sort of heroes. "You came all this way in that vehicle? That's amazing." And then one guy exclaimed, "We'll give you all of these Jeeps for your Land Cruiser!"

I quizzed them about the road they came from regarding difficulty and the distance to Highway 410. A guy said, "If you got this far you won't have any trouble getting out of here. We're on channel 7 so listen on your CB and we'll keep track of you until we get out of range. But don't worry, you'll make it fine." With that, we bid them farewell and eased the TLC down the hill.

The road into the valley had some steep switchbacks, so tight I had to stop and back up and go forward again to make the turns. Then we crossed over a rockslide with football-sized boulders and then a stream with no bridge. At one point, I was forced to cut down a tree because the space was too narrow to fit through.

Suffice it to say, we made it to the highway and stopped for a celebratory kiss. We then headed up to Paradise Lodge on Mt. Rainier and obtained a room for the night. It was good to be safe again and to be at Paradise was an extra bonus. The next morning we walked the trails nearby and enjoyed the marvelous array of wild flowers.

On the way home, we pondered our off-road adventure. When Sandy said, "Never again," I painfully recalled other times when I had overextended the thrill factor. I remembered the little rubber boat crossing Puget Sound in a storm and the camping fiasco on our honeymoon. Why can't I learn to ease into things so she will have a chance to acquire the taste for adventure?

I tend to go too far too fast and create so much stress that the experience leaves a bad taste. I expect too much from my companions who haven't had the benefit of previous exposure. I put them in dangerous or extreme situations and abruptly jerk them up to my speed at once. Naturally, they are overwhelmed and uncomfortable.

It's a good thing we don't know everything the tomorrows will bring when we start off on the trail to Heaven. Like Christian in *Pilgrim's Progress*, we learn faith along the way through the various difficulties we encounter. Over time we grow in our understandings and confidences. We discover that God is able to keep us and that he will never leave us nor forsake us.

Day by day he leads us—sometimes through deep water and fiery trials, and sometimes along rose-budded ways. We may pass through narrow, steep, and bouldery terrain. The next day we may encounter pleasant flowery paths. At all times and in all places "he leads his dear children along."

Chapter 14

Hot Showers By
Cold Streams

I served on the Board of Trustees of a college in the Midwest. As a board member, I was encouraged to provide something of value for a silent auction to help raise funds for the college. Sandy and I decided to offer a three-day off-road adventure in our Land Cruiser. In describing the vehicle, we noted that it included an on-board heated shower.

Interest in our auction offering ran high, with bids coming in right up to the end of the event. Finally, a couple from California won the bid and we began making plans for an adventure the next summer. We knew the couple, having worked together in Indiana years before. This trip would be a great opportunity to reconnect.

On the set date in early July 1998 we collected them at the airport and drove them to our home in north Seattle where we finalized our packing. Bright and early the next morning we headed over Snoqualmie Pass on Interstate 90 to Ellensburg where we left the highway for the backcountry. Our goal was to travel on Jeep roads southwest until we reached Highway 410. Then we would continue on to Mt. Rainier and back to Seattle.

During the trip the topic of the on-board shower surfaced repeatedly. I'd say, "If we camp by a stream or body of water, I'll hook up the shower and we can try it" (clad appropriately, of course). But water eluded us as we drove deeper into the barren wilderness.

By the time we reached 410 and Rainier, it was too late. When we arrived back home, we hooked up the shower in our driveway and tried it. With umbrella in hand, our guests stood under the flow of water.

Here's how it works: One end of a short hose is place in a stream or body of water (or a bucket) and the other end connects to a hose on the Land Cruiser. This hose goes to a water pump that draws water from the source and forces it through a heat exchanger and out a showerhead that is mounted nearby.

The heat exchanger is a tubular unit that is warmed by the engine's hot water flow. When the shower water passes through the center of the unit it is heated by the surrounding metal tube and flows out and through the showerhead nice and warm.

I have used the shower on several occasions when I've been alone in the wilderness. I recall one time I was camped by a stream near the Canadian border and hooked up the apparatus. The Land Cruiser was nestled in thick forest and I felt reasonably safe taking a shower in daylight. I may have had music on the stereo as well. No one, I'm pleased to report, interrupted my revelry.

One time the dealership where I purchased the Land Cruiser put the vehicle on display at an open house event. People would stand around and look at the various accessories and wonder why that showerhead was on a pole. I'd tell them about the shower and they'd roll their eyes. So I'd fire it up and use a bucket of water to show them how it worked.

From time to time people learn about my Land Cruiser shower and poke fun at me. They think it's weird that I'd have something like that. I invite them to give it a try. Others are curious and want to see how it works. Some people even want to stand under the flowing water. Whatever else it is, the shower is a mighty fine conversation piece.

By the way, you don't have to own a Land Cruiser to have an on-board shower. I'm sure you could figure out a way to install one on your Ford, Honda, or Chevrolet. Consider the possibilities!

So what's the point in all of this? For one thing, the Land Cruiser could serve as a portable baptismal unit for those who accept sprinkling as an acceptable mode. I'm kidding, of course. However, I do like the idea of the shower as an illustration of God's forgiveness and cleansing power.

Second, the mobile shower reminds me of the song, "There Shall Be Showers of Blessing." God is always ready to pour out his blessings of grace and goodness upon us.

Chapter 15

Dumb Things I've Done

I once toyed with the idea of writing a book titled, *99 Dumb Things I've Done.* I thought it would be a relaxing read and maybe even a tad entertaining. I could add a brief application at the end of each chapter to make the book more worthwhile.

I picked the title out of the air and wondered if I could actually come up with 99 episodes that contained an element of dumbness. I started a list and was surprised when the number shot past 99! I thought, *this is incredible. I had no idea my life included so many blunders.*

Life is a mixture of experiences, some worthwhile and others questionable. Maybe I should change gears and come up with a book titled, *99 SMART Things I've Done.* That, I decided, would be far more difficult. And even if I could produce such a book, I suspect the reader would quickly lose interest. I could see the book gathering dust on a shelf, or ending up as a white elephant gift.

This is not to say that remarkable stories of amazing exploits or inspiring tales of sterling behavior belong on the shelf. Wholesome biographies are wonderful treasures to read and reread. But for light reading there is certainly a place for pie-in-the-face self-depreciating accounts. This is especially true when the tales provide a modicum of life application to help the reader gain insight into his or her own journey through life.

At this point, it may help to define what I mean by "dumb." I do not mean dumb in the sense of uneducated or mentally challenged. I mean an act or decision that, upon reflection, would cause the culprit to blurt out, "I'm such a dummy!"

If you've read my earlier books on life lessons, as well as this one, you would recognize a plethora of "dumb things" from my personal experiences. So why a separate chapter devoted to five dumb things when nearly all of the chapters provide examples of behavioral blunders? Well, maybe I just need to expunge more of these gaffes from my memory bank.

No. 1 — Unhelpful Gestures

I was around six when my dad cut a gash under his big toe while working in the yard. Concerned, I followed him into the bathroom where he groaned and moaned and tried to doctor himself. Wanting to help, I knelt down to inspect the wound. Before he knew what was happening, I took hold of his big toe and lifted it upward to check things out.

If there was ever a moment when my dad could be excused for using a string of bad words, it was then. Yet, even in his pain he controlled himself. I instantly knew my error and immediately excused myself from the bathroom. A stern lecture followed later that day.

Dumb Things I've Done

Speaking of big toes, years later I was in the backyard of the parsonage trying to find and plug a hole in the fence to keep out the neighbor's cat. I quickly discovered an opening at ground level where the house and fence came together. Standing there in my flip-flops, I saw the unwanted creature nearing the hole in order to once again enter our yard to care for its bathroom business. Seizing the moment, I made a kicking motion toward the hole to discourage the cat. Unfortunately (at least from my standpoint) my left big toe missed the opening and smashed into the side of the house, bending the toe and nearly ripping off the toenail.

What happened next was somewhat inconsistent with what one might expect of a reverend. Hopping around the yard, I released a string of condemning comments on the offending animal, which by now was long gone. Then I limped into the house and sought sympathy and medical care from my compassionate wife.

Another unhelpful gesture occurred after pulling into a parking lot to climb Mt. Si near North Bend, Washington. When I got out of the car, I noticed a man trying to push his car backward. I went over and said, "Here let me help you." He said, "I'm just stretching my muscles before hitting the trail."

I walked away chastising myself. My embarrassment was compounded when I tried to explain my gaffe to my friend who had watched the brief episode.

Dumb things and ignorance seem to go hand-in-hand. Perhaps that is a clue in warding off unhelpful or unnecessary gestures. Jumping in to help someone may be the dumbest thing we can do.

Unless clearly an emergency, we might do well to pause, look over the situation, and determine how we might be most helpful. That's a principle, I think, we can also apply to our personal desire to interest others in spiritual matters. Before rushing forward with quickly formulated words or deeds, we might first apply the pause principle to get the lay of the land and seek God's guidance in what, if anything, we should say.

No. 2 — The Young Caddy

My dad was not a golf fanatic, but he did have his own clubs and spiked shoes. I'd guess he went out on the links a dozen or so times during the year. When I'd ask if I could go along, he'd say, "You're too young, son,"

Finally, at age 10 or so, I received the okay; Dad said I could be his caddy. He explained my responsibilities, including the role of bag carrier. I felt really important.

Golf day arrived and we drove to a public course a few miles from our home. Three of his friends met us there to make the foursome (plus me). I saw little carts buzzing along and asked, "Can we get a cart, Dad?" He mentioned something about cost and how walking provided exercise.

He put the bag on me and adjusted the strap so the bag wouldn't drag on the ground. As instructed, I stood off to the side and watched the four adults tee off toward the first green. I walked with my dad to his ball where he took another club from the bag and smacked the ball again. All of the balls were on the green when Dad called for me to bring the putter. Putter? I had no idea, so he came over and showed me the right club.

Then I walked onto the green...and suddenly stopped. There on the grass was a shiny dime. I went over and picked it up and announced to the men, "Hey, look! I found a dime!"

Four grown men groaned. One of them took the dime from me and placed it back on the green. My dad explained the error of my ways and I did not pick up another coin for the rest of the game, though I wanted to.

Even now, as I look back, I realize what a dumb thing I did. Yet I acted out of ignorance and no real harm was done. It was a learning experience and I'm sure the men had a good time telling others about the young caddy who picked up a coin on the green.

Dumb things happen along the way of life and the best we can do is to learn from them and move on to the next green. And if nothing else, we provide others with a smile or two.

No. 3 — My Embattled Sister

I'm guessing that most young boys with a sister feel duty-bound to tease her incessantly. For example, I cannot count the number of times I poked Stephanie and made faces at her in the backseat of our car while on a family outing. I would provoke her mercilessly until she loudly complained to the driver in front: "Make him stop, Dad!"

There would be threats from the driver and other harsh words. More than once the car would jolt to a stop and my dad would assume his role as the dispenser of justice.

It is true that my sister and I could get along famously, and I'd always come to her rescue if she was teased by anyone else. That domain belonged solely to me.

One of the most opportune teasing times occurred when she and I were home alone. I'd chase her through the house with a worm or garter snake, or maybe a squirt gun. Her best defense was to run into the bathroom and lock the door. In a few moments, I'd pretend to be bored with the "game" and head for the backyard to play. I'd open and close the door noisily and then sneak back to the bathroom and hide next to the door. Eventually, Stephanie would slowly venture out, only to squeal when I'd jump into view with a Tarzan yell.

One time, she ran past me and headed for the kitchen and the backdoor. She opened the door and ran out, slamming it in my face. Unfortunately, the glass window in the door crashed to the floor.

At that moment, brother and sister became the best of friends. Our calamity drew us together. We knew what would happen when Mom and Dad came home. Together, we cleaned up the mess and vowed to share the blame for doing such a dumb thing.

Isn't it interesting how a tragedy or misfortune can bring people together? Strained friendships can once again become vibrant when shared difficulties arise. This is true even though only one person suffers and the other is compelled by compassion to reach out and repair a broken relationship. Dumb happenings can have positive outcomes.

No. 4 — Burning Toast

I placed four pieces of bread under the broiler in the oven to make toast. It was snowy at our mountain cabin, and jam-covered toast seemed like a good thing to have with my coffee. I was alone for a few days, so my menu choices were rather simple.

After arranging the bread, I crossed the kitchen to a little built-in desk to check my email. Several messages had arrived and I began to read and reply. While typing away I detected a faint smell. I brushed it off as something coming from the wood-burning fireplace in the living room.

Soon the odor intensified and I decided to get up and look around. Only then did I remember the toast. When I looked at the oven, smoke was pouring out. Precisely at that moment the smoke alarm sounded. I grabbed a hand towel, pulled open the oven door, scooped up the smoking black bread and rushed it to the porch. I then opened two doors and the kitchen windows to air out the place.

Frustrated with myself, but not willing to surrender, I took four more pieces of bread and once again started the toast-making process. Then I returned to the computer.

After several minutes, a lightning strike of remembrance hit me and I leaped up and rushed to the oven...only to find smoke pouring out again. I grabbed the towel, scooped up the smoking bread, and deposited it on the porch. How dumb can one guy be?

Once again I reached into the dwindling loaf of bread and pulled out four pieces and placed them on the broiler pan. This time I stood there and waited for enough browning to occur before flipping the bread. Then I waited for the second side to brown and turned off the oven. Four pieces of nicely browned toast, ready for jam.

Now, do you think this is the first time I have done something like this with toast? It pains me to say that a similar thing happened before, and before that. I also ruined a teapot or two.

What moral can we gain from my toast-making fiascos? For one thing, don't trust your memory. Second, use the timer. And third, make sure you have plenty of bread on hand!

No. 5 — The Mattress Fiasco

I wanted to try out my new hiking boots, so Sandy and I headed for Mt. Rainier and the trails in that area. After a day of gawking at the scenery and trekking a few trails, we headed eastward toward Yakima. We planned to stay at a motel on the way and then drive to our home in Ellensburg the next day.

It was quite depressing to pass motel after motel with "No Vacancy" signs. Finally we came to an older looking place with a neon sign announcing, "Vacancy." The lateness of the hour instructed us to snatch a room no matter how crummy the place or what the cost.

One room was available so we grabbed it. After carrying our stuff inside, I sat on the bed to check out the condition. We like a firm bed and this one was softer than a bag of marshmallows. "Never mind," I told Sandy. "We'll just pull the mattress off the springs and put it on the floor. That ought to take care of the firmness issue."

I put my boots in the closet and we got ready for a good sleep. Unfortunately, the lumpy mattress and drafty floor made for a miserable night.

The next morning we packed up, eager to be on our way. Sandy, who always likes to leave a motel room as nice as we find it, wanted my help to get the mattress back on the bed frame.

"No way," I said. "They can do it themselves. We paid good money for a lousy night and I'm not going to pretend the bed was just fine."

So we left and headed for home. As we were pulling into our driveway, a horrid thought introduced itself: I left my new boots in the closet! A second sickening sensation quickly followed the first: We left the mattress on the floor!

I called the motel to check on the boots and got an earful about the mattress. The woman thought we had used the room for two additional persons without paying for them. She was upset and I sheepishly tried to console her. I hung up, got in the car, and drove all the way back to the motel to retrieve my boots, and to grovel my way through an apology for leaving the mattress on the floor.

I meekly assured her that no one else shared the room with us. I mentioned that we needed a firm bed because my wife was pregnant and my back was acting up. Still, she exhibited a sour attitude.

With a final apology and boots in hand, I got back in the car and retraced my drive home. Along the way I chided myself for being so dumb as to leave my boots behind and for insisting that the mattress remain on the floor.

Sometimes we can let the irritations of life prod us into doing dumb things. We make snap decisions and later discover that our hurried actions cost us additional money and time. More importantly, by our careless deeds and attitudes, we leave behind a negative impression. Better to pause and think things through before doing something dumb.

Chapter 16

Dad, the Ranger, and the Rifle

I was six or seven when we drove across the country to visit my mother's relatives in Indiana. During our stay, my uncle took me to a store in town that had just about anything you could imagine.

He said, "Roger, I'll buy you anything you want in this store. Just go pick it out and I will get it for you."

Instead of searching out an expensive item in the toy section, I made my way to the display of toy guns and selected a wooden rifle. "I want this!" I declared.

He paid the cashier a couple of bucks and we returned to grandma's house. I could hardly contain myself as I showed off my new fake rifle. I was every bit as thrilled as Ralphie in *The Christmas Story* when he received his BB gun. I was the happiest, proudest, toughest cowboy in Petersburg, Indiana. I seem to recall, however, that my grandmother lacked a bit of enthusiasm for my new "weapon."

When it was time to head back to Seattle, my dad packed the toy gun along with the luggage in the trunk. Our route included a trip through Yellowstone National Park and so we headed in that direction.

Arriving at the park entrance, we stopped at the gate and a ranger collected a fee and asked us a few questions. He said, "Do you have any firearms in the car?"

My dad said, "No."

But I knew differently and immediately lunged forward from the back seat exclaiming, "O yes we do! There's one in the trunk!"

My dad's efforts to explain that it was just a toy gun failed to impress the ranger. In order to continue into the park, Dad had to unpack the entire trunk and produce the wooden rifle. During the search, I remained in the back seat, quaking in the awareness that I had committed an egregious error.

I will not try to reconstruct the conversation that followed as we drove into the park, except to say that I was appropriately chastised.

Does the following application work? A toy testimony—a wooden witness—can fail to accomplish good for the kingdom of God. We are called to be authentic, real, and loaded with the power of the Holy Spirit. We are not to play church or run around like tin soldiers, brandishing fake firearms.

Rather, we are in the midst of a battle where the real bullets of temptation fly. We are engaged in a life and death struggle against the spiritual forces of evil. So keep your weapons of prayer, the Bible, and a holy life oiled, loaded, and ready for battle.

Chapter 17

Free Christmas Trees

When we lived in Icicle Canyon we'd walk through our property and select a Christmas tree early in December. I'd cut it and place it in a holder in the living room. Sandy then worked her magic decorating the tree. It was always an ooo-ahhh creation. During the month we'd enjoy it, as would our family and others who dropped by for a visit.

However, by January the tree would be dry and dropping needles. It was my job to discard it. Since we always had a slash pile out back, I'd toss the dead tree on the heap for burning in the spring.

What do city folks do with their used non-artificial Christmas trees? The Boy Scouts may offer to collect trees for a donation of, say, $5. Or maybe the local sanitation service provides Christmas tree disposal.

When I was around seven years of age, I had a different view of used Christmas trees. After the holidays, I noticed several trees in the alley behind the houses on our block. They were probably there for the garbage truck that came through once a week.

To my young mind, this seemed a terrible waste. These trees had only days before graced the homes with cheerful beauty, rising above an array of brightly colored presents. And now here they were free for the taking!

So I began collecting the trees. One by one I dragged them to our garage and stood them up along the inside wall. And where I found no trees, I went to the door and knocked, "Hi, I'm collecting old Christmas trees. Would you like me to take yours?"

People were so very nice and it felt like Christmas all over again as I continued to amass my collection of trees.

What a coup! These probably cost $8 or $10 and now they were mine. With every tree I felt richer, more important. Ah the rewards of accumulation and ownership. By the end of the day, at least a dozen trees adorned our garage.

Then my dad came home from work and his lack of enthusiasm for my entrepreneurial success caught me by surprise. It is fair to say he was not a happy camper. I learned swiftly the error of my ways…and the problems of disposal.

I don't remember how my dad handled the situation. He may have made me return every tree to the place where I found it. Maybe he rented a trailer and hauled them to the dump. Whatever he did, I assure you I didn't collect trees the next year.

The trees I gathered those many years ago can represent various things to us today, such as the lifeless "treasures" we accumulate. Our possessions can look so wonderful dressed in tinsel and light; but in reality they are dead trees dropping needles in the living rooms of our hearts. They are destined to be tossed on the fire.

Free Christmas Trees

Periodically, it's a good idea to take stock of our inward adornments. What are we accumulating? How strongly are we attached to our possessions? What really counts for time and eternity?

Chapter 18

Sleds, Bikes, and Bruises

During my youth we lived in a modest home on a steep street on the lower north side of Seattle's Queen Anne Hill. Between our front yard and the street ran a concrete sidewalk the length of the block. Between the sidewalk and the curb ran a strip of grass four to five feet wide.

When winter snows came, this strip of grass provided the perfect runway for sledding. We'd go to the top of the block, climb onto our sleds, and fly like the wind down the hill.

The street did not continue past our block. Instead, it ended and formed a "T" with Florentia Street, a busier road running perpendicular to our street. Are you following me? What I want you to picture is a sled zooming down the hill and spilling into the yard on the other side of the street running east and west.

Because of possible traffic on Florentia, it was incumbent upon the sled driver to brake sufficiently before entering the street. We got pretty good at this by rolling off the sled near the end of the run. At times, the sled would continue across the road and into the neighbor's yard.

On one occasion, my good friend Burt and I decided to double up and make the run together. We were seven or eight at the time and he was a little bigger than me. Because of his superior size, we agreed that he would be on the bottom and I would occupy the top.

This was actually our first run that winter and we were particularly interested in the mound of snow near the end of the run. We envisioned ourselves hitting that pile of snow and enjoying a brief airborne ride before bailing out of the sled.

After shoving off at the top of the hill, we braced ourselves as we came to the mound and hit it with more than the normal speed of a single rider. The moment of impact is fixed in my mind because at this point we discovered that the mound was not snow, but a pile of sand lightly covered with a dusting of snow. When we hit sand, the sled slowed abruptly.

As we slid forward off the sled, Burt's mouth encountered the metal steering apparatus and he immediately lost two front teeth. I, however, escaped with only minor bumps and bruises. The sled was no worse for wear. The lesson? Things are not always what they appear to be.

Now you would think such a fiasco would cure us from such crazy stunts. Not so. A few years later we tried something similar with a bicycle. This was a kid-sized bike with normal tires and a braking system that required pushing down on the back pedal to slow the "vehicle." We decided to double up and ride down the street, applying the brakes in time to keep from entering the cross-street at the bottom.

I don't recall which one of us was at the controls, but I do recall that the braking system did not perform adequately. We entered the street and barely managed to turn enough to ride out the trip without further incident. Had we met a passing car when we entered Florentia Street, one or both of us might not be around today to talk about it. In any case, that was the last time we rode double down First Avenue North.

A more dramatic example involved a school friend who was delivering newspapers on Queen Anne Avenue, one street to the west of our house and three or four blocks up the hill. As he rode his bike down to the next block, his chain came off and he descended the series of steep streets out of control and with mounting speed.

I was walking on the sidewalk doing my own paper route on Queen Anne Avenue, half way up the block from Florentia. I suddenly heard the yells of someone in danger and turned to see a school friend zooming straight down the hill on his bike. Time froze. I saw the fear on his face, the chain dragging on the ground, his paper bag flying in the wind.

With a sickening feeling I realized he was about to cross Florentia Street. At the bottom was a wooden blockade to provide a minimum amount of protection for those who lived in the houses across the street.

I watched in horror as the bicyclist crossed Florentia and hit the curb on the opposite side, narrowly missing the blockade. The bike and rider did a complete somersault and smashed onto the sidewalk leading up to the front door of a house.

I stood there in shock and disbelief. Finally, gathering my wits, I ran down the rest of the hill to where my friend lay groaning. Neighbors poured out of their houses and someone called for an ambulance. His pant leg was ripped open and a large gash ran the length of his calf. I shuddered when I saw an exposed leg muscle.

If I recall correctly, he had 90 stitches and recovered fully from the ordeal. The memory, however, still haunts me. What a miracle that he lived to again deliver papers!

One more bicycle story: This one finds me on a touring bike—skinny tires and multiple gears. Here it is in real time: I'm rolling westward along Nickerson, a busy street near Seattle Pacific University. I come to a stretch of road with a gentle downward grade and peddle to gain more speed.

It's a four-lane road and cars are parked sporadically along the curb. My mind wanders as I enjoy the speed and the wind on my face. It's great to be keeping up with traffic.

Something catches my eye and I turn my head left to check it out. No, it's not a girl. Maybe a car going the other direction. Whatever it is I move my gaze back to the roadway in front of me just as I smack headlong into a parked car.

I skid over the car and land at the opposite end on the ground. The damaged bike lies on the street to the side of the car. I shake myself off, take a deep breath, and walk the rest of the way home with my bent bike in tow. It could have been so much worse.

Why do I get a pass on these and other accidents? I don't know, except there must be a divine hand at work somehow. I have been spared on too many occasions to chalk it up to chance. And not me alone, but I can tell you of friends who came abruptly to death's door only to be turned away. For example, I think of a good friend who rammed his car into a tree while driving 90 miles an hour. Or the time he broke his neck on a trampoline and recovered without any ill effects.

I do not understand the providences of God—why some are spared tragedy and others seem to dwell in the "Valley of Deep Darkness." It is a mystery that will only be revealed in the eons of eternity. One thing I do know, however, is that God watches over his children with loving care. He is with us in the valley of suffering, even when we place ourselves there by a dumb act or decision. He is our Shepherd and we are the sheep of his pasture.

Chapter 19

Spike Jones and
Me

Spike Jones and the City Slickers brought levity and laughter to the musical scene of the 1940s and early '50s. Noted for their parodies of popular songs and their humorous desecration of classical music, Spike kept true to his motto, "They write 'em and I wreck 'em."

The talented musicians would begin a grand tune like the William Tell Overture and soon turn it into a wild cacophony of whistles, gun shots, bird calls, cowbells, auto horns, and a variety of sneezes, hiccups, snores, and belches.

For some unexplainable reason, these maligners of musical favorites caught my fancy and I hooked my young-teen wagon to this comedy sensation. By the time I was in the seventh grade I was going strong doing pantomimes of Spike Jones "music."

I'd take my place in front of the audience and someone would place the needle on a 78-rpm record and away I'd go. With near perfect synchronism, I'd mouth the words and act out the sound effects. I was an instant success and began moving swiftly up the ladder of show business notoriety—at least in my little world.

I performed for assemblies at grade school and provided entertainment for birthday parties and other social gatherings. I was a hit at our youth group retreats and in front of friends who would egg me on when the radio played a Spike Jones rendition. I must have loved doing it because I was never remunerated for my efforts—except maybe an extra piece of cake now and then.

For a while it seemed my popularity knew no bounds. Kids and adults liked me because I would act stupid to music and make Spike "come alive" on the stage. I was lip-syncing before it became vogue.

For sound effects, I'd push on my nose to mimic a fog horn and point my forefinger to my head to feign a gun shot. Every odd sound of the band found a place in my repertoire of gesticulations.

Surfing the Internet, my wife found a used commemorative DVD of Spike Jones and the City Slickers. She ordered it to see what kind of a nut I used to be. We made popcorn and sat down to watch the collection of old television shows featuring the master of musical mêlée.

As we watched the antics I recalled many of the numbers I had pantomimed as a young teen. Interestingly, three things did *not* happen:

First, I did not feel the slightest urge to stand up and revisit the past by performing for my wife. Second, neither of us laughed or giggled. And third, we did not rush to the phone to invite our friends to come and see the DVD.

After dutifully watching the whole thing, we ejected the disk and went on to something more entertaining. Even now as I think about it, I can't believe I gained even a fleeting moment of popularity by acting out the various sounds of the Spike Jones band. I must have been really hard-up for friends.

Hmm. Now that I think of it, maybe people were laughing at my stupidity instead of my artistic performance. Maybe they were pretending to like it just to keep me acting silly. Could it be they were simply making fun of me?

And my folks? I can't recall even the slightest encouragement. They were probably embarrassed to own me as a son.

Wait! I just now see Mr. Rankin's face and a broad smile. Surely my seventh grade teacher wouldn't let me make a fool of myself. Oh, and I must factor in my sister's seemingly sincere encouragement. Maybe I really was funny way back then.

I'm not sure why I departed the pantomime business, but it likely had something to do with cars and girls and wanting a manly persona. In any case, I think my last live performance was a youth group event in high school. After that I abruptly hung up my comedic ways…at least until seminary when they came back with a vengeance. But that's another story.

One of the applications I derive from my pantomiming adventures relates to our propensity to mimic those we spend time with. Quite unconsciously, we assimilate their gestures and voice inflections over time. We may even find our thinking affected by repeated contact with certain people. A parent, a coach, a teacher, a close friend—these all have more influence on us than we may like to admit.

The Apostle Paul knew this when he exhorted the Philippians to pay attention to their role models. He told them not to follow the example of earthly minded people, but rather to imitate those who love Jesus and who are looking forward to his appearance.

Aping Spike Jones and the City Slickers was all in fun and I don't think I've suffered any ill effects. But had I been more serious about my "craft," I might have made a string of poor decisions that I'd later regret. I'm glad I chose to hobnob with those who seek first the kingdom of God and who truly know how to have a good time.

Another application pertains to the stage we inhabit day by day. We are on display, as it were, and we can either amuse the onlookers with frivolity and empty living or we can inspire them with words and deeds worthy of imitation. We can be actors playing a role or we can live our lives authentically.

A third application deals with the need we all have for appreciation and acceptance. I liked the popularity I gained from my comedic antics, though I realize now how shallow and transitory it was. It is far better, as someone said recently, to focus on playing well before an audience of one, the One who delights in our obedience and applauds our faith.

We can be like those who, as Jesus said, so live that when the curtain falls they will hear, "Well done, good and faithful servant."

Chapter 20

Camp Bloopers

I was around 13 when I played the bugle at a Christian youth camp. I had learned to do this as a Boy Scout and even earned a merit badge for my efforts.

The hardest part of that camp was getting up before anyone else and playing reveille. Actually, it wasn't the getting-up part that bothered me most, but the challenge of having to play when my lips were swollen with sleep. I remember carrying the bugle out to the flag pole, making motorboat sounds with my lips to limber up. I stretched my mouth and contorted my lips. I made buzzing sounds into the mouthpiece.

Try as I might, I was never quite ready when I launched into the wake-the-dead bugle call. One could always count on at least one significant sour note, the kind of error that would adorn conversations at breakfast and throughout the day.

During that week of daily humiliations, I made one further error that guaranteed me a place in the Bible Camp Idiots Hall of Fame.

Every afternoon the camp store opened and we were allowed so much time to purchase pop, candy, and other sugar-infested foods. Awash with money from my paper routes, I loaded up on goodies one day and stashed them high in the rafters of the barracks I inhabited with a dozen other boys.

That evening, I went looking for a candy bar and discovered to my horror that all of my treats were gone. Stolen!

I immediately challenged some of my cabin mates to come clean. Their denials infuriated me further, sending me trembling with rage to the counselor.

He gathered all of us boys together in the barracks and lectured us on having respect for personal property, honesty, and the Golden Rule. He said we were not leaving until the guilty person or persons stepped forward and returned my candy. Silence.

Then one of the boys, peering way up into the rafters said, "Hey, what's that stuff up there?"

I looked and, behold, there it was…everything I had purchased and exactly where I had left it earlier that day. I had not climbed high enough for the candy bar and had mistakenly assumed someone had stolen my goods.

Do you have any idea how popular I was at that moment?

Not only did the entire camp have the bugle bloopers to munch on, they now had the filet mignon of my false accusation.

Sometimes life just seems to go downhill. We get ourselves into hot water and then jump into the fire. We go from bad to worse.

I made it through that week of camp…as well as other humiliating episodes during my life. In fact, sometimes I think

I've had more than my share of groaners. Maybe you feel that way about yourself.

I am learning, finally, to look upon these unpleasant occurrences as character-building opportunities. It must be working because my wife calls me a "real character."

There ought to be a verse in the Bible that says, "Count it all joy when you make a fool of yourself, for in so doing you learn of your own imperfections and, hopefully, develop forbearance for other blooper-prone persons when they sound a wrong note or mistakenly rush to judgment."

So don't be too hard on yourself when you take a humiliating tumble. Just remember that *in everything* God works for good to those who love Him.

Chapter 21

Bumper Cars and the Police

For 30 years Seattle was home to one of the biggest amusement parks on the West Coast. Located just north of the city line on the shores of Bitter Lake, this 12-acre "million dollar pleasure resort" boasted the "Big Dipper," a wild rollercoaster twisting every which way and running more than a half mile. The rides and other attractions of Playland were meant "to banish jaded nerves, nagging thoughts and worries, and to apply instead wholesome recreation and relaxation."

The park flourished in the '50s, partly because of my attendance and the paper-route money I spent. One of the rides I particularly liked was called "Dodgem Cars."

While I enjoyed the Big Dipper, the Roll-O-Plane, the Shoot the Chutes, the Giant Whirl, and the Red Bug Speedway, I gravitated to those little bumper cars and the excitement of ramming friends and strangers alike.

I'd see a helpless victim across the way and push down my accelerator to build up maximum ramming speed. Then, wham!

I'd smack into the other car and send it skidding. The rider would verbally chasten me. All in fun, of course.

I'd get rammed, too. Sometimes the jolt would come as a surprise and I'd feel fleeting pain as my neck jerked.

Traffic jams happened all the time. A mass of bumper cars would clog up the works and the operator would have to walk over and undo us. I hated the jams because they took away precious time for ramming.

The frenzy of banging and smashing and crashing suddenly stopped when the ride timed out. We'd sit in our cars feeling powerless. Then we'd leap out and run to the back of the line for another ramming experience.

The park is long gone, but the memories remain. I don't recall any accidents or evil deeds associated with my trips to Playland, nor do I recollect anything extraordinary in the Tunnel of Love. I just remember fun.

When I became 16, I acquired my first car—a '46 Ford. With it I transitioned into a whole new dimension of existence. The car provided freedom and thrills and temptations unknown in earlier years.

We lived on Queen Anne Hill—one of seven hills in Seattle. Several of us high schoolers had cars and we motored around the hill looking for adventure. Somewhere along the line the idea of the Playland bumper cars surfaced. We decided to modify things a bit and reduce the rams from all-out crashes to light taps—as in playing tag. I think we also may have used water balloons and other means to designate, "You're it!"

Three or four of us would meet together in our cars and set location boundaries for the game. The one rule: Don't wreck another guy's car. The "it" car would wait 60 seconds and then charge off to find any of the others. Once he tagged another car, that vehicle became "it" and raced around looking for the others. I can still recall zooming down back alleys trying to outrace my pursuer. I'm sorry about the crumpled garbage cans.

Somewhere along the line my car lost its muffler and floorboards and brakes. Yes, brakes. Our high school was on the top of the hill and we lived near the bottom. Getting home from school in one piece challenged my driving skills. I would come down in low gear (no muffler) and scrape the curb with the sides of my tires and use my emergency brake and, if needed, jam the manual transmission into reverse.

During that year of irresponsible driving, not one of us was injured—nor anyone else in our path. Evading the police, however, was a different story. One time when we were chasing each other around the hill, a police car caught up with the last person and cited him for reckless driving. Unfortunately the guy in front of him circled around to see what had happened to his pursuer and nearly ran into the police car. He, too, was cited. Both guys lost driving privileges for a time—hence our decision to take up other forms of entertainment.

In my senior year I decided to sell my '46 Ford and buy a newer one. I made a list of everything wrong with it and placed it in the window—"100 Things Wrong With This Car." Problems included broken windows (every one of them), dents all around, no back seat, ripped upholstery, broken radio, no brake lights, no brakes!, no muffler, and on and on. Price? $100. Amazingly, a fellow student bought it!

I don't know why I'm telling you all of this because it makes me look like a dope. But maybe you can learn something from my stupidity. Here are four possibilities to prod your thinking:

1. *Words can hurt.* We can ram others with destructive comments and create long-lasting scars. Even seemingly innocent word-taps spoken at the wrong time can jar a person's equilibrium. Instead of accelerating in our wish to get even, or even coasting into a disagreement, we can put on the brakes and steer clear. We can avoid accidents by living carefully and obeying the rules of kindness and consideration.

2. *How we live affects others.* We can race around endangering the peace of others with our noisy ways, reckless attitudes, and self-absorbed behavior; or we can live peaceably in our communities. "No Man is an Island" is more than the title of a song; it's a fact of life. What we say and how we say it touches people we don't even know.

3. *Rules are good.* Just as road rules are meant for the safety of all, so the ordinances of decency and thoughtfulness contribute to a healthy family, church, workplace, and community. Showing off or endangering others by breaking the laws of good conduct not only reveal a wayward soul, but also short-sighted perspective. What goes around comes around and the offending party usually suffers unpleasant consequences.

4. *Let's hear it for the police!* Getting caught was one of the best things that happened for those two guys…as well as the other two of us. We all straightened up real fast and decided that our vehicular tag game was over for good. The same is true spiritually when the Holy Spirit convicts us of sin. We look back on those "citations" and revel in God's goodness and mercy.

Bumper Cars and the Police

The Word of God and the loving comments of a pastor, parent, or friend can be used to arrest us and awaken our need for confession and repentance…and open us to the forgiving grace of Jesus Christ.

Chapter 22

Spanking and Other School Memories ℰ⌢

I attended North Queen Anne Elementary School, two blocks from our house. I remember nothing about kindergarten, except building forts with wooden blocks, taking naps on my own blanket, and having a daily snack.

My first grade teacher was a bully. She didn't take guff and she meted out swift punishment to any offender. I recall the day she brought an offending student to the front of the class, laid her across her lap and proceeded to spank her before us all. That sure wouldn't happen today! One thing for sure, none of us acted up in class for the rest of the year.

My second grade teacher was an older woman, Ms. Wall. She had one distinguishing feature: a foaming mouth. When she talked, saliva congregated near her teeth. When she sounded certain consonants, those sitting in the front row suffered a mild shower. Also, in that class, I recall each of us making cards and then passing them around on Valentine's Day. I think it was the first time I became aware that there was a female species (other than my sister).

Third and fourth grades are a blur, except that one of the grades belonged to Ms. Foot. I always thought that was funny because my mother's maiden name was Head.

My fifth grade teacher tried to keep me in line by reminding me that I should not bring shame upon my wonderful Christian parents. Occasionally, Ms. Deringer would threaten, "Do you want me to talk with your parents about your behavior?" I'd gulp and correct my behavior.

Sixth grade proved to be memorable for several reasons: First, we had a teacher, Mr. Mendenhall, who was tall and lanky and walked with a limp due to an earlier bout with polio. He was a no-nonsense guy who failed repeatedly to see the humor in our youthful antics.

The second reason I recall sixth grade was the "coming of age" of several class clowns. They kept things interesting.

And third, most of us had been together since kindergarten and had polished our skills at bringing teachers to the brink of a nervous breakdown. Parenthetically, a good friend at another school did in fact participate in the emotional undoing of his sixth-grade teacher.

Back to Mr. Mendenhall. One of his first efforts to control the class included "The Commotion Club." This brainchild was designed to punish students who acted up during the day. If one of us was deemed worthy of a place in this club, we would join other members after school at the chalkboard where we wrote (in cursive) the same sentence over and over, according to the extent of our misbehavior.

For example, I remember having to write, "I will not create a commotion in class" a hundred times. Because of limited chalkboard space, other members might be assigned a certain number of sentences in a notebook at their desks. This included Raymond who had marked up his wooden desk with deep gouges. He had to write, "I will not destroy school property" several hundred times.

The more we caused difficulties in class, the longer our membership tenure in The Commotion Club. Eventually, the whole thing backfired on Mr. Mendenhall when membership in the club became a badge of honor. Normally upright students began to act up just to gain entrance in the group.

As the days progressed, most of the class were still in the classroom after school, writing on the chalkboards or in notebooks at their desks. This is why the teacher let the club die and went on to a more positive approach.

To give you an idea of the antics we contrived, imagine an old clock on the wall with a noisy tick-tock, tick-tock. It has a glass cover which has to be opened to move the hour or minute hand. The teacher leaves the classroom for a few minutes. Jackie, seizing the opportunity, takes a pointer stick and stands on a wooden chair and reaches up to open the clock door. She moves the minute hand forward 10 or 15 minutes. Then she tries to close the clock door and in the process breaks the glass. At that moment, Mr. Mendenhall appears and Jackie finds herself in big trouble.

Seventh grade turned out to be a positive experience. Our young teacher, Mr. Rankin, related well to us and knew how to keep us interested in the curriculum. We all thought the world of him.

Now come with me to Queen Anne High School. Since there was no middle school, once we reached eighth grade we entered high school. Whereas grade school was a hop, skip, and jump from our house, the high school was located on the top of Queen Anne Hill. That meant hiking a mile or so up the hill to go to school.

My first memory of QAHS was gym class and the bigger-than-life teacher, Coach Hinkle. When I showed up for class he asked me to go to the supply room and get a left-handed football. "Yes sir," I said and headed to where I thought the supplies were kept.

About half-way there I asked myself, "What is the difference between a left-handed and a right-handed football?" I stopped walking. I asked a guy walking by, "Is there such a thing as a left-handed football?" He thought for a moment and replied, "I don't think so."

I walked back to the gym and Coach said, "Where's the football?" I said, "There's no such thing as a left-handed football!"

He got a big kick out of that and brought it up more than once that year. I just groaned and scolded myself for being so dumb.

Another memory from high school relates to Mr. Burmaster and a mechanical drawing class. One day the class was particularly unruly and there were giggles and needless coughs as the teacher tried to explain something at the chalkboard. When his back was to the class, one of the students snorted a laugh. Suddenly, Mr. Burmaster (knowing who it was) grabbed an eraser, whirled around, and fired it at the offending student.

Spanking and Other School Memories

The student saw the missile coming and ducked just in time. The eraser hit the next student in the face, one of the outstanding students in the class. An awkward moment followed, during which the shaken teacher expressed a mixture of contriteness and exasperation.

When I shared this memory on the high school Facebook page someone who was also in the class corroborated the story. Others added additional stories of a similar nature. Apparently, Mr. Burmaster was somewhat unconventional in his disciplinary methods.

One more memorable event; probably the most devastating experience of my high school career. I am referring to Ms. Gorrell and algebra class. It was my junior year and I was more interested in having fun than learning mathematics. The teacher, a rotund woman of serious demeanor, indicated that I had better get my act together or I would fail the class. I took her warning with a grain of salt.

When grades came out and I looked at my report card I couldn't believe my eyes. I had never seen an "F" on any paper or report card and I nearly went into shock. My anxiety gained momentum as I faced having to tell my folks about the failing grade.

The silver lining occurred when I and a good friend from another school (who likewise failed algebra), took summer school together and both received a "B" grade. Our teacher just happened to be a guy from our church who was committed to helping us pass the class.

My senior year went much better, partly because of the jolt I previously received from Ms. Gorrell. I suppose I should have gone back to her with a bouquet of flowers.

There are many other stories during those high school years, some I would love to forget. In fact, I find it interesting that most of my recollections contain an element of the absurd or some degree of misbehavior. I don't seem to remember normal happenings.

The Bible urges us to exercise our forgetter. In one of his letters, the apostle Paul writes about forgetting the past and pressing on to what lies ahead. I think we can apply this admonition to those events of the past that we regret and that perhaps left emotional scars.

And while we seek to rid our memories of negative thoughts we can also coax forward pleasant remembrances of persons, places, and events that contributed to our lives in a positive way. Living well means that we avoid dwelling on the past and instead focus our attention on the future and what we can do to create memories we will later be pleased to recall.

Chapter 23

City Slicker

I was visiting a friend who lived on a farm in a peaceful valley 10 miles from the logging town of Shelton, Washington. Though also a young teen, he was a "man of the earth" and I a "city slicker." Determined to indoctrinate me in the ways of farm life, he taught me—among other things—how to drive a tractor, ride calves around the barnyard, skin a steer, and shoot a 12-gauge shotgun.

The latter lesson took place in back of their property along a stream. We were looking for ducks and crept along the water's edge like two stalking braves. We came to a place where a log crossed the stream and I hopped on it and walked gingerly out to the middle. I had the shotgun and he had an inspiration.

"Take a shot at the stump over there."

I planted my feet and steadied the gun at my shoulder. It was my first time at this and I was a bit nervous. I inquired, "How close do I hold the gun to my shoulder?"

He said, "About two inches forward. That way you won't feel a thing when you pull the trigger."

I held the gun loosely, sighted the target, pulled the trigger, and landed in the water.

While he roared with laughter, I crawled out of the stream a wiser young man.

The story reminds me of a second narrative that also includes a firearm. A year later, at 15, I worked on the farm with my friend during the summer. I think I received $1 per hour. The education I acquired, however, far surpassed the few dollars I accumulated.

This episode included a .22 rifle. I don't remember where I obtained the .22, but I may have borrowed it from my friend's older brother. In any case, it had good sights.

Four or five of us took our guns down the road a few miles to an abandoned barn owned by one of the boy's parents. We tumbled out of the vehicle and looked around for something to shoot at.

An apple tree stood nearby. The lower fruit had been picked by deer, but some juicy apples hung from the higher branches.

In my John Wayne manner, I said, "I think I'll knock down one of those apples and take a bite."

They stood around watching as the city kid raised his rifle, took aim, and fired. In the back of their minds they may have recalled the story of my prowess with the 12-gauge shotgun the previous year. Perhaps they were thinking of the way I bounced up and down on a horse or the dumb questions I asked. No doubt they were looking forward to another source of mirth.

Miraculously, I hit the twig holding the apple and down it came, nearly into my hand. I picked it up and took a bite.

Then I looked around at my gawking friends. "Anyone else want an apple?" I asked.

"Yeah, I'll take that one over there at the end of the limb," said one, baiting me to make the impossible happen twice.

"No problem." I raised the rifle and pulled the trigger. The .22 slug went out into space never to be seen again.

Not only did I miss the stem and the apple…I failed to hit anything else we shot at that day.

It was a simple fluke that I downed the apple in the first place and since that day I have chastened myself for failing to put the gun away after the apple fell, leaving the gawkers guessing.

I did a similar thing 10 years later when I played golf for the first time with my wife's father near Detroit. He was an avid golfer, hitting the links two or three times a week. Feeling very much the novice, I avoided his invitations to play. I eventually weakened and he put together a set of extra clubs and we went to play nine holes.

On the second hole, I hit a hole-in-one. Honest. He had never done this himself and just couldn't believe that I was able to walk up to that ball and smack it a hundred yards into a little hole.

Again, I failed to capture the moment and lock it up as a legacy. I could have feigned a sudden bout of dysentery or heart pain or a migraine…anything to cease the game right then and there. But stupidly I swaggered to the next tee-off and attempted a repeat performance.

Need I say that I missed the ball on my driving swing? And need I add that it took me 14 strokes to sink the ball at the next green? Oh, and need I say that I tripled Judd's score?

Let us beware when we shoot an apple out of a tree or hit a hole-in-one or accomplish some other unusual feat. We may not be as special and skillful as we might like to think…or cause others to think. Our "achievement" may simply be a fluke, a once-in-a-lifetime oddity.

Instead of gloating, it is better to direct the attention to God in every happenstance of life. Better to place our confidence in the One whose aim is impeccable every time and who never needs two strokes to sink the ball. Better to glory in his redeeming deeds and awesome acts. Better to brag on him and praise his name.

And when oddities happen, or even well-practiced achievements, wisdom counsels us to avoid taking the least bit of credit. Better to humbly gather the oohs and aahs into a bouquet and lift it up with thanksgiving to our Father in heaven.

Chapter 24

Ranger Roger

I have written previously about my 1957 summer stay at Granite Mountain Lookout in *Hikes, Flights, and Lookout Stories*. In another book, *Saga of the Red Truck* I wrote about fighting a forest fire the next summer near Dingford Creek as a backcountry patrolman. Now, in this current book, I want to add one more story about the summer of 1958.

While I enjoyed my time on Granite, I found myself envying the two guys who lived at Camp Brown, a guard station several miles to the north and west of me. They patrolled two river valleys and the Taylor River Campground.

While I was stuck at one location, they were "out and about" having new experiences nearly every day. One of these guys, Merlin, was a student at Whitworth College in Spokane, Washington—a Christian school much like Seattle Pacific College where I was to attend.

Merlin and I decided to apply for the Camp Brown positions for the summer of 1958. We were hired and when June rolled around we attended fire camp and then headed off to this little outpost 20 miles from the paved highway.

The two-room cabin was located 30-40 feet off the dirt road with a green lawn in front. Further north from the guard station, two river drainages met at the campground and from there flowed past the cabin as the Middle Fork of the Snoqualmie River. The river continued until it connected with the South and North Forks and then, as the Snoqualmie River it flowed over Snoqualmie Falls on its way to Puget Sound and the Pacific Ocean.

Anyone who wanted to camp at the Taylor River Campground or hike any of the area trails or fish the streams and rivers had to pass by our little cabin. Some would zoom by kicking up dust and others would stop and inquire about this or that. During the day, one of us would usually stay at the station while the other patrolled "his" river. Merlin was assigned the Middle Fork drainage above the campground and I had the Taylor River valley.

It was a great summer job for two young men and we had many interesting experiences. One of the downsides, however, was driving our own cars. Merlin had a Volkswagen and I drove a '49 Ford. The roads, particularly up the Taylor River valley, were rocky and tough on tires. I had one flat tire after another. In fact—and this is gospel truth—I had 18 blowouts during that summer.

The problem was that I kept replacing the bad tires with cheap retreads. Even though the Forest Service paid us a per-mile rate for using our cars, the money was far from adequate to keep me in tires. As the summer wore on my bank account dwindled.

Finally, with only a few weeks of summer left, I reached the tipping point. I drove my car into the Forest Service parking lot in North Bend and walked into my boss's office where I announced I would *not* be driving that car back to Camp Brown.

I nearly fell over when he said something to the effect, "No problem, George. You can use one of the trucks with a fire suppression unit. Check with Fred out back and he'll go over the pump instructions and give you the keys."

As I drove back to the guard station I could hardly believe my good fortune…and the ease with which this had occurred. I thought to myself, "You big dummy! Why didn't you ask for a truck two months ago?"

I don't know to this day whether I had simply hit the ranger on a good day or whether he knew from my earlier reports about the blowouts that I had reached the end of my rope…or whether all I needed to do was to ask. Whatever the reason, I ended the summer in style.

Sometimes we go through life suffering needlessly because we don't bring our needs to our heavenly Father. We go from blowout to blowout trusting in our own resources and ignoring the provisions God has for us.

Joseph Scriven, the hymn writer, put it like this: "O what peace we often forfeit, O what needless pain we bear, all because we do not carry everything to God in prayer."

Sometimes the road is rocky and rough. Sharp stones of criticism and pointed spikes of doubt puncture the weak fabric of failing faith. Chuckholes of discouragement and the broken glass of hurt feelings can penetrate and flatten our joy and hope. We lose mobility.

There are many hazards on this road called the Upper Way, and we don't need to wait for the umpteenth blowout to get serious about our spiritual condition. We can act preventively by claiming the provision of God and by clinging to his all-powerful Presence.

Chapter 25

Living Off the Grid

When our children were young, Sandy and I would pack them into the van and treat them to a "one-tank vacation." This meant finding a place requiring a half-tank of gas to get there and the other half to get back home to Seattle. The fact that our vehicle was fairly economical to run helped us reach a variety of beach and mountain locations.

One of the places we particularly enjoyed was Leavenworth, Washington, a Bavarian theme village a hundred or so miles to the east. We had a favorite motel and we enjoyed the sights and activities geared for family fun. As our trips to Leavenworth continued, the thought emerged that maybe we should invest in a little cabin near the town. We could develop family memories and perhaps someday even turn the property over to our kids to enjoy with their own children.

The thought simmered on the backburner until the day Sandy and I walked into a real estate office and revealed our aspirations to an agent named Jim. I explained we wanted something easy to maintain, near town, and reasonably priced. I said, "We'd like a place that our family could enjoy for decades. It could even be vacant land where we could build a cabin."

We looked through his packet of listings and found nothing of interest. He said, "I'll keep you posted. If something shows up that rings a bell, I'll send you a note."

For three years we interacted with Jim. And three times we actually made offers on 20-acre parcels that provided pleasing views of the Leavenworth valley. The first two fell through because our offers were unacceptable, but number three clicked. The seller accepted our offer and we signed the commitment papers. We incorporated several contingencies, including proof that water could be reached on the property.

We talked with a well driller and waited for the results. Time dragged by and the settlement date drew near. Finally, only a week remained before the contract expired and I became insistent that the driller do the job ASAP. It was Saturday and he agreed to get up there on Monday to see if he could find water.

The next day it started to snow and it continued unabated for a week. The road was impassable for the drilling rig and the expiration date came and went. Our realtor sought to calm me, indicating that "these things happen. I'll just have the seller and agent extend the expiration date." That did not occur. In fact, the seller raised the price $50,000 and put the property back on the market.

We felt cheated and disappointed. But then we realized what had happened. We had been praying that God would shut the door if this property was not for us. And now, here was a clear answer to our prayers. Our grumblings turned to gratitude as we saw the hand of the Lord in what had occurred. We continued our search for the *right* place.

In the early spring of 1999 Sandy and I took some friends from Illinois on a sight-seeing tour of the Washington Cascades. We left Seattle and drove over Stevens Pass on U.S. Highway 2 through Leavenworth and then south over Blewett Pass until we hit I-90 for the trip back to Seattle over Snoqualmie Pass. The all-day event included a stop in Leavenworth to allow the ladies to shop in the Bavarian village.

To pass the time, Bob and I drove up Icicle Canyon to see the jagged spires of snow-covered mountains. We returned to Leavenworth a little early and I asked if it would be okay to stop by the realtor's office for a quick visit.

Bob stayed in the van while I went in to say hi to Jim. I asked about any new properties for sale and he said, "Nothing yet, but I'll let you know if something pops up." Then, just as I was leaving, I turned and said, "You know, Jim, it doesn't need to be vacant land. We'd be open to look at a little cabin close to town."

With that bit of encouragement, Jim said, "Hey, I just thought of something! A place up Icicle Canyon just came back on the market and the owner cut the price $100,000. He needs to sell and it might be something that would fit some of your criteria." The more he described the place, the more interested I became—22 acres on the Icicle River, a custom home built with Douglas fir, off the utility grid, and surrounded by spectacular scenery.

I told him about our out-of-town guests and that I needed to confer with Sandy. I said, "I'll get back to you in a few minutes."

Bob and I then drove to the prearranged pick-up place and I jumped out to talk to Sandy privately about my visit with Jim. Behind the van, we talked about our guests and decided to go on with our tour and maybe drive back over the pass in a day or two for a look at the property. Bob's wife had not yet climbed into the van and overheard our conversation. After I said we would continue with the tour, she raced around the van and said, "Oh let's go see the house now! I love to do this sort of thing."

With that, I called Jim and asked if we could see the place now. He contacted the owners and then called me back and said, "I'll meet you at the driveway of the property."

As we drove the eight miles up Icicle Road to the property we wondered aloud, "I don't see any houses. Do people actually live up here?"

Jim was waiting at the driveway and led us up the 600-foot road to the house. The owner was on the roof shoveling off snow and his wife was digging around in the dirt planting bulbs. They greeted us and gave us a brief tour of the house and detached garage. We could not walk the property because a foot of snow still covered the ground.

Sandy and I were both smitten with the beauties of the outdoors and the charm of the house. It was clear a few things needed to be done, but it certainly had "location, location, location."

Two days later we returned to Icicle Canyon where the owners and the two realtors met with us to discuss our long list of questions. We talked about the challenges of living off the grid and issues relating to winter and the wildlife. At the end of our discussion, we told our realtor that we would call him before we arrived back home and give our answer regarding the property.

Sandy and I had been praying earnestly about the property and asking for the Lord to keep us from error. We prayed again as we left Leavenworth for home. Yet, instead of apprehensiveness, we felt an amazing peace. Sandy wasn't sure how she would handle living in the wilderness but felt the Lord was leading us forward and so she said, "Let's go for it!"

Twenty minutes after leaving town we called Jim and said we had decided to buy the place. I asked him to fax the papers to my office and said we would sign them and send them back ASAP.

We moved in a few months later and that was the beginning of a 15-year adventure. For seven years we commuted back and forth most weekends while I continued my publishing business in Edmonds (north of Seattle). I sold my business in 2006 and we moved to our wilderness home fulltime for the remaining eight years. I might add that Sandy surprised herself by taking to wilderness living like a duck to water.

If you're familiar with this area of the Cascades, we were located north of the river and between Cannon and Cashmere Mts. with an unobstructed view of 10,000-foot Mt. Stuart—the only place in the canyon where one can view this mountain. We were surrounded by the Alpine Lakes Wilderness Area, including a one-mile buffer zone of National Forest property.

Our property sat at the foot of the famed Enchantment Lakes, which included the highest lake in Washington State. Our closest neighbor on our side of the river lived one-half mile away.

One thing we liked about our home in Icicle Canyon was the energy independence. While powerlines in the city or other areas of the county might be knocked down by storms or other hazards, our power source was ongoing and dependable. We were free of public utilities and monthly electrical and natural gas concerns and bills. We found life off the utility grid to be wonderfully liberating.

Our system included a diesel generator, a back-up gasoline generator, a few solar panels, a deep well, propane for heat and refrigeration, and a septic system. We had a 1,500-gallon cistern for water, a high capacity gasoline water pump and a couple hundred feet of fire hose. We had snowmobiles for the snow and an all-terrain vehicle (ATV) for getting around the property the rest the year.

During our 15 years at Alpenglow (the name we gave the place) we had a forest fire rage through our property (miraculously sparing our buildings), landslides that cut off road travel, rolling rocks from above, and various encounters with rattlesnakes, bear, and other wild animals. More than once we had a bear look us over through our windows and we had to keep the screen door closed so a bear wouldn't wander into the house. I think we saw every type of animal in the forest during our time at Alpenglow, including a wide assortment of birds.

I had only one serious run-in with a bear. While I was standing on the back porch, a bear was maybe 30 feet away. Suddenly, he charged me. Since the porch is only a step up from the ground, it's easy for man or beast to get there.

When I saw the bear coming, I threw my arms about and yelled and basically put on a wild display of human craziness. That brought him to an abrupt stop a few feet in front of me. He had never seen anything like that before. I glared at him and he studied me. With great force I declared, "This is my porch and you are not coming up here. You have the whole forest to live in so leave my porch alone."

I could almost see the wheels turning in his head, as though counting the cost of tangling with a maniac man. Then he wheeled around and ran like a scalded dog into the bushes. Sometimes I wonder what would have happened had the bear attacked me on the porch. Another time I came close to a bear cub with its mother a mere 50 yards ahead of me. As I quietly backed away, the cub ran to its mom and the two headed up the hill behind our house. I don't think my crazy man routine would have worked in that setting.

I have a picture here in my office of a year-old bear standing just a few feet from the back porch, hugging a choke-cherry tree. I could have almost reached out and touched him. He seemed so docile and harmless. His mother, a cinnamon-colored black bear, was up in the tree feasting on the cherries. She also seemed unconcerned by my presence. Yet, I was well-aware of the harm the two of them could do if provoked.

During our 15 years at Alpenglow, we had loads of visitors and small group retreats for pastors, church boards, planning committees, and men from Union Gospel Mission in Seattle who were trying to overcome addictions. We never charged any of the groups, feeling that the Lord had given us Alpenglow for others to enjoy as well as ourselves.

A teenage daughter of the previous owners was given an assignment at school to locate, identify, and take pictures of 100 different wildflowers. She found all of them at Alpenglow. That gives you some idea of the uniqueness and kind of beauty that surrounded us day after day.

After the forest fire of 2001we began the long and tedious job of cleaning up the mess. A small logging operation harvested 10 logging-truck loads of partially damaged trees, and we did the rest. I felled more than a thousand trees, cut wood for winter use, and (with Sandy's help) split and stacked wood, cleared the land, planted new trees, and burned more than a hundred slash piles. At every opportunity we worked hard to return the property to a healthy and attractive condition.

Working with a contractor, we also built additional structures, including a fuel shed, additional storage, an extension to the house, a self-contained retreat area above the lower garage, and a new second garage with three spacious bays.

Sometimes we were asked whether it was cheaper to live off the grid or to pay for utilities in town. Basically, the answer depends on usage. Some years it would be less and some years more. I did a little figuring one time and it appeared that the costs were basically comparable. However, even if town living was cheaper, we considered energy independence a prized value.

It would take several books to relate all the experiences we had at Alpenglow. Suffice it to say, we were blessed with good health and many enriching times in every season of the year.

Living in the wilderness means that you sometimes encounter people who need help. For example, one winter evening we were sitting at the dining-room table when we heard footsteps on the stairs leading up to the kitchen. I opened the door and found a man and woman about ready to drop. They said they had just walked about seven miles after their car got stuck up Icicle Road in the snow. (They should never have driven up there!). One large dog was with him. Two smaller dogs were left in the car.

I got my gear on and took them to the Land Cruiser and helped them in. The dog's paws were so cracked and bruised that I had to help lift him into the vehicle. During the winter I kept chains on all four tires and used the Cruiser to get up and down our driveway to reach our parked pickup on the main road. As I headed up the canyon, I noted the layer of rough ice on the road and realized how the dog had torn up his feet.

The couple did not have a flashlight and there was not much moonlight for them to see. I was surprised they made it all the way to our place, which they didn't know was there until they saw our lights up the hill to their left. Had they missed our lights they would not have seen another light for five miles.

We arrived at their car and I pulled it out of the snowdrift. I let them go ahead of me down the canyon in case they got stuck again. When we got to our driveway, he stopped and walked back to the Cruiser. He held out some money and asked me to take it, thanking me profusely for helping them. Of course I declined and said something like, "Give thanks to God." To which he replied, "Oh I do, I do!"

There are so many spiritual and practical lessons packed into those years at Alpenglow, and so many times when I could have been snuffed out by a falling tree or other hazard. For example, I often climbed part way up the steep mountain behind our house with a few supplies stuffed into a small backpack. I liked to find a suitable place and sit to enjoy the wonders of the view. I'd take out my little stove and brew a cup or two of coffee.

Some mornings I'd hike up to "Breakfast Rock" and prepare a hearty breakfast.

On one occasion, I followed a makeshift trail that took me through a narrow V-shaped area just wide enough at the bottom for a boot. Giant boulders walled the trail. Just beyond this was a car-sized boulder that leaned out over the trail. You had to duck to pass under it.

On this occasion I bent forward to allow my pack to miss the overhanging rock. Then, thinking I was beyond the boulder, I abruptly stood up. My head smashed into the giant Granite rock, knocking me backward into the V-shaped section of the trail, pinning me to the ground.

I couldn't move and I didn't know whether my head was bleeding or whether I had suffered a concussion. I also wondered whether I was near a rattlesnake den.

I prayed and squirmed around until I could get sideways and shed the pack. Then I righted myself and stood there a few moments doing damage assessment. The pain subsided and I started back up the trail for my destination, thanking the Lord for his protection.

Wilderness living is like a slice of life that we all encounter along the way. We are led and protected in ways we never comprehend. We are children of our Heavenly Father and he daily watches over us and helps us when we call upon his name. Do we give him thanks for his watchful care? I want to be like the man on Icicle Road who answered, "Oh I do, I do!"

Chapter 26

When Trees Fall Elsewhere

Sandy went on a mini-vacation with our daughters and I was left to fend for myself. The weather was nice, so I decided to go out and drop a few dead trees. I've probably cut down 1,000 trees on our property since the 2001 forest fire, and I think I'm getting the knack of it. Cut 'em down, buck 'em up, save the good stuff for winter fuel, and burn the rest in slash piles.

I had three chain saws—a big one for big jobs and two smaller ones for the smaller stuff. Like I say, I'm a regular logger. I took one of the smaller saws with me and drove down the 600-foot driveway in my ATV to a tree near the gate. It was a dead Maple, 14-16 inches in diameter—a piece of cake for the Echo 18-inch saw.

I stood under the tree and looked up, noting what seemed to be a decided lean away from the driveway. I made my undercut on the opposite side of the tree to assist the direction of fall. Then I cut into the front side and watched for the tree to begin its fall away from me.

Not all trees cooperate…and this one had a mind of its own. For some wacky reason, the tree pulled around and came toward me and the driveway. I stepped lively to the side and helplessly watched as the falling tree crashed down across the ATV. Not a glancing blow mind you, but a direct hit.

I examined the ATV. Axels seemed okay, but the carrier rack on back was seriously bent. The padded seat was slightly damaged as well. I turned on the key and the motor came to life. I removed the tree and drove the vehicle up the driveway and back. While it looked like a crumpled crab, most everything worked fine.

Sometimes you plan your work and work your plan, only to discover that things have a way of changing directions. Your expectations and good intentions fall by the wayside. The tree drops elsewhere and you have to adjust your plans.

Now come with me to the backside of our property where I again drove the ATV to a dead tree. This time I had a little trailer attached for hauling the wood rounds back to the shed for splitting. I positioned the vehicle in a safe spot and walked over to the fir tree with my chain saw.

I studied the large tree and determined my cutting plan. I would fell it straight down the hill where I could buck the rounds easily. As with the maple tree, I decided not to use wedges to guarantee the direction of fall.

You already know the outcome. The tree managed to twist and fall in the wrong direction. However, instead of hitting the ATV, it crashed on the trailer, flattening it to the ground.

So at this point you are thinking *I do not want Roger to cut down any trees near my house, nor by my car, nor by me!* I understand…but really, my success rate is pretty high. Still, there are those occasions when trees simply fall elsewhere.

Life is like that. Things change unexpectedly and we must alter, compensate, modify, revise, vary, and amend our plans.

Jesus faced the same thing. He would heal a demon-possessed person and sternly charge him not to talk about it openly. But his plans were thwarted more than once by these overly enthusiastic heralds.

Another example: After his disciples returned from their missionary travels, Jesus took them off to a lonely place to get some rest. That's as far as they got, because the crowds caught up with them and the solitary place became a beehive of activity. Instead of rest, the disciples were once again pressed into service. The plan backfired. The tree fell elsewhere.

What is important here is not that an unexpected change occurred, but that Jesus took advantage of the change and turned it into a stepping stone for advancing his kingdom. He used the occasion to feed a multitude with a little sack lunch and thus taught his disciples about compassion, divine provision, and spiritual multiplication.

It was not Paul's plan to spend two years under house arrest in Rome, but when it happened he seized the occasion to preach the gospel until it penetrated the royal guard. His negative circumstance actually served to advance the gospel.

That's the key: Grasping every unexpected happening—even a damaging event—as an opportunity to experience the faithfulness of God and to advance his kingdom in this world.

Trees fall elsewhere, but one thing remains the same, one truth stands firm: The sovereign Lord of Hosts is with us to take the "unexpected" and turn it to his benefit…and ours.

After several years of cutting down trees and burning slash piles, we finally caught up with the mess left from the 2001 fire. The remaining challenge was a stand of 30-40 cottonwood trees, each towering 70 to 80 feet. Some of them measured 25 inches wide. I had been dreading these trees because they had been dead long enough for the trunks and limbs to become brittle.

The most dangerous feature of cutting down trees like these is the chance that the vibration of the saw or other disturbance near the ground could cause a large limb to snap and fall, or worse, cause the top of the tree to break off and come crashing down.

While I used a hard hat for much of the tree-felling work, I sometimes wore a baseball cap instead. On one occasion, while I was sawing, a high limb broke loose and came down like a rocket and hit my left upper arm with a glancing blow. It didn't break the skin, but it did hurt and left a swollen welt. Fortunately, I was wearing a long sleeved shirt and was standing fairly close to the tree.

The next day, the exact same thing happened with another tree. Same arm, same place. But this time the skin broke and I suffered a few scratches. In both cases, I was concentrating on cutting the tree and unaware of the falling missiles until they hit me.

Had either of these large limbs conked me on the head, I would have been knocked out or worse. And, yes, I know I should have been wearing my hard hat. (I donned it after the second limb fell. I'm what they call a slow learner.)

In looking back at these close calls, I consider myself quite lucky...or, I should say, blessed by the protective hand of God. Even though I failed to protect myself adequately, He chose to keep those limbs from hitting me directly on my head or shoulder.

Sometimes, God helps us in spite of ourselves. Maybe we fail to protect ourselves with morning prayers, only to realize that he stepped in and helped us through a fix later in the day—without our even asking!

These times of gracious intervention cause us to love him more...and to pray more out of gratitude than obligation.

Our heavenly Father knows what we need even before we ask. He who watches over us neither slumbers nor sleeps. We are his children, the sheep of his pasture. He whose eye is on the sparrow, watches over you and me. Indeed, eye has not seen nor ear heard the number of times he has stepped in and, unbeknown to us, rescued us from tragedy.

O the stories we will hear from the angels in heaven!

Chapter 27

Caught In the Current

For years I envied fly fishermen who could stand in the middle of a stream and not get wet. Those hip waders seemed like such a good deal.

So finally I bought myself a pair. To try them out I drove eastward from Seattle into the Cascade Mountains. Leaving Interstate 90 behind, I followed a dirt road up the Middle Fork of the Snoqualmie River. I stopped at a broad stretch of river and surveyed the situation.

Though moving swiftly, the water appeared to be shallow. Nearly quivering with excitement, I donned the waders, strapped on the creel, hung a small net from my vest, adorned my hat with extra flies, grasped my fishing pole, and headed into the water. I'm guessing the opposite shore was about 50 yards away.

I immediately experienced the elation I had been dreaming about. Here I was standing in icy water—dry. Others may be confined to the shoreline, but not me. I was in the river, among the fish. I felt a surge of freedom and power.

The water flowed strongly. The steady pressure pushed against my legs. I quickly learned to slide one foot among the slippery rocks and get good footing before moving the other foot forward.

The fishing could wait. I wanted to experiment, to test my new equipment. Check out the limits.

The further I went, the deeper the water and the stronger the force against my legs. I picked my way carefully, moving forward by inches.

Twenty-five yards and I halted my advance. No way could I make the other side. The question became, could I make it back?

Gingerly I turned around. Though I stand more than six feet and weigh a whole bunch of pounds, one mistake and I'd turn into a reluctant rubber raft.

For the sake of adventure, I'd like to report that I lost my footing, floated downstream two miles, encountered a large bear fishing mid-river, wrestled the monster and prevailed, removed my waders and swam to shore—just before reaching Snoqualmie Falls. But that's not the way it happened.

For several minutes I just stood there leaning against the current, frozen with fear. I presented a picture of someone caught in the currents of life, trying desperately to stand against the flow.

Life is like that rushing river. Faddish philosophies and harmful allurements push against our noble commitments. Temptations swirl about us. The world would lift us and carry us away—down, down until we tumble over the falls into the bottomless pit.

But God's Word admonishes us to stand. On several occasions the Apostle Paul says, "Stand fast." In one place he writes, "Be watchful, stand firm."

No matter how strong the current, we are called to keep our feet on the Rock and withstand the pressures of the day. Praise God, we are not alone! The Lord is with us to strengthen us and to help us stand. He is there to lead us safely to the other side.

With some careful maneuvering I made it back to shore… and gave thanks. I had been one small slip from catastrophe.

Today as you take another step forward against the mighty forces of evil, do so in the strength of our Lord. Keep one eye on the distant Shore and the other on the dangers and opportunities at hand. Be careful, persistent, and joyful…and do some fishing.

Chapter 28

The Timeshare Pitch

Disneyworld is expensive. That's why we decided to attend a sale's pitch for a timeshare. The lady at a special booth in the motel lobby said the 90-minute presentation even included a free breakfast. Not a bad deal: breakfast, 90-minutes of hype, and a two-for-one ticket to Epcot Center. We made a reservation to attend first thing the next morning.

We had no intention of buying anything, but since the offer indicated "no obligation" we decided to give it a whirl. And besides, if it was a fantastic deal, maybe we would consider a timeshare unit in our future plans. At least we'd give them a chance to ply their wares.

We arrived at the massive complex a few minutes early and drove up to the guard station for entrance permission. Beaming with good nature, the sharply dressed man pointed us toward the reception center. "Have a great day!" he called as we drove away.

We parked and walked in. A dozen couples and singles milled around. There was coffee, but I didn't see breakfast. We got in line at one of the windows for processing.

A cheerful woman asked several questions about our interests, our family, and our economic condition. We were told to take a seat and wait for one of the reps who would assist us further. "Have a cup of coffee," she said.

The room was active by now with reps introducing themselves to various customers. The air was charged with smiling faces and hearty greetings. A woman called our name, mispronouncing it awkwardly. She apologized and told us that this would be a very special occasion for us.

We followed her outside and boarded a golf cart for a quick ride to the presentation building. More enthusiastic than a well-honed car salesperson, she pointed out various features of the property as we drove along. Swimming pools, magnificent landscaping, beautiful buildings—we took it all in.

She pulled under the canopy of a centrally located building and we hopped out and went through the automatic doors to a classy bank of elevators. Up we went a few floors to a large open eating area with at least 80 four-person tables scattered around. I spied a buffet table off to the side and took heart.

She led us to one of the corner tables and then encouraged us to help ourselves and bring our food back to the table. As we ate, she unloaded a sales pitch that would make any sales professional sit up and take notice. Occasionally, I would interrupt with a question or try and redirect the one-sided conversation. It was as though she was moving through an invisible script and wanted to cross the finish line before I finished breakfast.

I tried my best to interject cautionary words about our lack of desire to obtain a timeshare condo. I said we were willing to hear the proposal, but that our primary purpose was to gain the discount tickets to Epcot Center. My words went right over her head and she plowed on with her planned remarks.

When we finished eating, she moved us back toward the elevators where we descended and took a cart ride to a model unit. Naturally, it was well appointed and had a great view of Disneyworld beyond a sparkling lake. Two or three other couples were milling around the unit with their handlers while we were there.

Then it was back to the cart and the dining room and the table where her notebook awaited our return. She shifted into high gear. She spoke of our family and how they would benefit from our foresight and how it would be so neat to bring our friends to visit now and then. Surely we would be the envy of everyone who knew us.

She took out her pen and began scribbling figures to convince me of the financial benefits of timeshare ownership. She had answers for every objection. I noticed how she tried to get us to agree on a particular point and then to build on that agreement to move us another step closer to a positive decision.

I said, "You're really good at this; how long have you been working here?" I think she said eight years. In any case, she confirmed my assessment that she had some seniority in the system and had selected my name after reviewing the information on the initial questionnaire.

Finally, with great effort, we brought her to the understanding that we were not going to buy anything. We were there solely to see the place, learn about the process, and get the free ticket.

Defeated and with obvious disgust, she rose and went over to a person who seemed to be monitoring the various tables.

He came over and she introduced him and then disappeared without a goodbye. We never saw her again.

The sharply dressed man (suit and tie) sat down and tried to pick up the pieces. He offered us a free night's stay that night and a further presentation the next morning. He also had a "special" pricing deal for us if we wanted to proceed. We told him thanks but no thanks and that we were ready to go. He made a notation on our information form and asked us to wait a moment.

He went and spoke to another man who came over and sat down. He said this was an expensive process for them and that they expected people to make a positive decision. I told him we were done and ready to go and that I wanted to know how to bow out gracefully. He wrote on our form and told us to take it to the exit desk at the main building where we started earlier. I glanced at my watch—two hours.

When we left, we were directed down the back fire exit stairs and out to a landing where a van was supposed to take us back to the place where we started. No van. No signs. No personnel.

We walked over to the back entrance of the welcome building and presented our information form to a woman at a window. She asked a few questions and reluctantly, it seemed, provided a coupon for Epcot Center.

Then, when we walked over to the "exit" door leading to the lobby and the parking lot, we encountered the eighth and final representative (including the lady at the motel): This one looked like a bouncer at a night spot. He said he had one more option for us to consider. I don't recall what it was because by that time little plumes of smoke were emitting from my ears. I wanted out of there.

With coupon in hand, we drove to Epcot Center and parked in the "back 40." After walking a half mile (it seemed) we got in line at the ticket counter. When I presented the coupon, the ticket person looked puzzled. I tried to explain and that only intensified the confusion. My blood pressure rose.

I asked for a supervisor and the "problem" was readily solved. Apparently the one we had encountered at first was a new employee and didn't know about such coupons.

In any case, we spent the next several hours touring the park and trying the rides. After one space journey ride for "astronaut trainees" we battled upset stomachs, reminding us of our age and abdominal sensitivities. Despite the many interesting things in Epcot, we found our conversation returning to the morning's experience at the timeshare complex. It was a powerful lesson on how not to win friends and influence people.

There are, of course, applications here not only for business and marketing, but also for presenting the gospel on a personal basis. We can push and pressure and appeal so earnestly that we cross the line of good manners and respectful behavior. We can turn off otherwise interested people by our hard-sell techniques.

What's more, if we pressure someone into a decision, we may gain another notch on our gun but lose in the long run when the "victim" gets away from our influence and rushes to reject the "defensive decision" made in an effort at self-preservation.

It's hard for a parent or friend to honor the dignity of an unbelieving person when so much is at stake. We know what's best and we try to overpower resistance with argument and admonition. We forget that it's the Holy Spirit's role to convince and convict.

It takes an ocean of wisdom to guide people into the truth… and much prayer. And not everyone follows our gentle appeals and personal example. Jesus lovingly tried to win the rich young ruler in Mark 10, but the man was bound by his wealth and went away sorrowful.

We are not contending for timeshares, but for an eternal home in heaven. The stakes are high. Yet the manner of our presentation can either draw or repel prospective believers. Let us follow the example of our Lord and treat people with dignity and compassion, honoring the profound power that is theirs to choose a place in heaven or eternity elsewhere. God help us to be wise as serpents and harmless as doves.

Chapter 29

Stuck In Coeur d'Alene

I stepped out of the pastoral ministry temporarily in 1969 to obtain a Master's degree in Counseling Psychology at Central Washington University in Ellensburg, Washington. I thought the added schooling would help me be a more effective minister in the years ahead.

However, when I finished and offered myself for reassignment, there were no suitable vacancies in the conference. We could go to a church in another state or conference, but decided against that. We began to consider other options.

As we prayed about this, we began to pack our possessions. We knew we were going someplace, but didn't know where. Boxes, taped and labeled, filled the porch, the kitchen, and living room; and yet we still didn't know where we were going or what we would be doing.

The phone rang. It was the publisher of the Free Methodist Publishing House at the world headquarters of our church denomination. He was calling to see if we might be interested in coming to Indiana as the editorial director. He would fly out and interview me in Seattle if I wanted to discuss the position. I think he had some other business in the area as well.

Editorial director? The guy in charge of acquisition, content, and correctness of all printed materials for the entire denomination? The thought both scared and puzzled me. I wondered how this would work for one who had been forced to take bonehead English in college. Yet, knowing that God moves in mysterious ways, we decided to proceed.

Sandy and I met the publisher at a popular restaurant near the University of Washington. The interview went well and he called me upon his return to Indiana and offered me the position. It seemed to us a clear answer to prayer.

It was hard to leave Washington State, but we took comfort in God's faithfulness and set our minds on the adventure before us. We sold our two vehicles and rented a 20-foot truck for the move. We packed it to the gills with boxes, furniture, and other belongings. Behind the truck we attached our dog trailer for the three dogs we took along. On top of the trailer's flat roof we secured furniture odds and ends and other awkward items that wouldn't fit in the truck.

As we drove eastward out of Kittitas Valley we wondered if we'd ever return. Indiana seemed as distant to us as India.

Seven-week-old Jonathan occupied a small cardboard box between us on the bench seat. It was early August with temperatures in the high 90s and the truck lacked air conditioning. Still, we had plenty of time to allow us to find a motel early each afternoon to get out of the heat and relax.

We were nearly to Coeur d'Alene, Idaho, when steam began pouring from under the hood. Then the motor stopped and we coasted to the shoulder of the road. With the help of the police, we were able to get a large tow truck to come and haul us into town. It was quite a sight—the tow truck followed by the truck crammed with our goods, followed by the trailer and the dogs.

At the Chevrolet dealer, we discovered that the motor had a cracked block and that it would take three to four days to get a new motor delivered and installed. There went our leisurely drive across the country.

A nice man with a pickup took us and our trailer to a cheap motel where we stayed for four days waiting for the truck to be repaired. It was a miserable time with no restaurants near, no transportation available, excessive heat, cranky dogs, and our firstborn infant son.

We wondered why this was happening to us. Did we somehow miss the Lord's will? We expected smooth sailing and all we got was choppy seas.

The disciples were obeying Jesus by "going to the other side" when they encountered a fierce storm. They thought he was unconcerned, distant, and detached from the crisis at hand. But he was right there all along and they soon learned they were completely safe with him.

Today, you may be rowing against the wind. Unexpected waves of difficulty may be crashing against you. You may think Jesus is unconcerned and detached.

God never promised us a rose garden. Sometimes we encounter fire and flood and fierce storms. Calm circumstance is not a good barometer of God's will. Four days in a miserable motel in Coeur d'Alene didn't mean we had missed our calling.

What counts most when we follow Christ is the quiet assurance that he is with us and that he is able to use the choppy seas of life to reveal his sovereign rule and faithfulness. His peace is the best indicator that we are moving in the right direction.

Chapter 30

And the Loser is...

After seminary I married my sweetheart and within two weeks we were living in the upperclassmen's dorm at Greenville College in Illinois. I was a faculty member, teaching in the Philosophy and Religion Department, and Sandy attended her sophomore-year classes. In addition to teaching a full load, I was also the head-resident of the dorm.

I think it was Thanksgiving time when the sophomore class arranged a hay-ride social at a local pig farm. We arrived just as it was getting dark and boarded the large hay wagon. The farmer used his tractor to pull the wagon around the farm. A rather large assortment of hogs loitered here and there and I'm quite sure we were all glad to be in the safety of the wagon.

When the ride concluded, we dismounted the hay. "Wait!" Sandy yelled. "I just lost my wedding ring!" The cool air had shrunk her finger and the ring slipped off as she slid down from the wagon. Car lights were directed to the area behind the wagon and several class members joined us on the ground as we searched for the ring.

After several minutes, I said, "We'll come back tomorrow when we have more light." I pushed a stake in the ground where we were searching so we'd know where to look upon our return.

The next day after church, the farmer and his wife joined Sandy and me at the search site. I had brought some string and long nails and we proceed to make a grid of squares that we could systematically search. Several of the huge hogs drew near with quizzical expressions—at least that is what went through my mind. Perhaps they were thinking hostile thoughts about us someday enjoying a sumptuous breakfast of eggs and bacon.

We started at the center and slowly worked our way outward, sifting through the loose hay and dirt. A gold wedding band blended well with hay, making it very difficult to spot the ring.

We were beginning to wonder whether one of the pigs had run away with the ring during the night. Would someone someday find the ring embedded in a shank of ham?

Suddenly, the farmer's wife jumped up and exclaimed, "Girls! I found it!" The farmer and I looked at each other. Girls?

That is not the last time Sandy lost her wedding ring. She once tossed a football and her loose ring went flying after it. But it is not Sandy who holds the loss record. I am far and away the champion in this arena. I have lost hearing aids, glasses, credit cards, books, important papers, wallet, phone, and yes, even a child.

The lost child episode occurred at Alderwood Mall in Lynnwood, Washington. I needed to get something at the mall so I decided to take my youngest daughter with me. Julia was four or five at the time. It was Saturday and we walked into the mall hand-in-hand. Julia was instantly enthralled with all the sights and sounds and strained at my hand to go this way and that. Somewhere along the line, she broke loose from my hand and walked beside me.

A few moments later, I looked down to check on her. Gone! I stopped and scanned all around me. She couldn't have gone very far. Panic began to well up inside me as I failed to spot her. I thought of child snatchers and what other harm could befall her.

I saw an information booth down the way and hurried to report a missing child. The person took my information and radioed the guards who were patrolling the mall. I was really getting worried and didn't know what to do.

Then came the radio message, "I've got the girl." I looked down the way and there was Julia, hand-in-hand with a guard, not having a care in the world. If you're a parent of a young child, you'll know exactly the relief I experienced.

On another occasion, I lost my shirt. It was a bad financial investment and I don't want to talk about it.

I've also lost my way more than I care to admit. There was the time I nearly landed at the wrong airport, and the time I hiked several miles on the wrong trail.

One of the most embarrassing losses occurred on a trip to Chicago. I was an independent consultant in charitable gift planning and working with a donor regarding a sizable planned gift. Wanting me to know more about his situation, he gave me a copy of his financials to look over before our next meeting.

During the flight, I reviewed the statements and then tucked them into the seat pocket in front of me. I planned to review them further after resting my eyes. My attention turned to other things and before I knew it we were landing at O'Hare. I gathered my belongings and left the plane with the other passengers.

It wasn't until I reached my room that I remembered the financial papers on the plane. A terrible sick feeling seized me. I immediately called the airlines and reported the loss. They checked the lost-and-found to no avail and told me that the crew cleans the plane thoroughly after each flight and discards any papers left behind. That didn't calm me and I fell into a dreadful fear as I envisioned someone finding the papers and using the information to invade my donor's financial accounts.

I tried to think how I could best break the news to my donor. I couldn't be sure that the papers were destroyed even though I told myself that was probably the case.

When I talked with the donor, I blamed myself profusely. Amazingly, he remained calm and thoughtful. There was no anger or blame or resentment. He knew how badly I felt and assured me his accounts would be just fine. The experience of losing such important papers still weighs heavily on me, even though it happened more than 25 years ago.

The whole idea of loss carries broad implications. Someone has said, "What you don't use, you lose." When we drop the habit of thanksgiving, we lose a positive frame of mind. We lose friends when we treat them carelessly. And, spiritually, when we grow cold in matters of prayer and faith, we lose insight and wisdom and the precious sense of God's presence.

Sometimes we must search diligently for what we have lost. And if we are blessed enough to find it, we must grasp it all the more tightly lest it disappear again.

Chapter 31

Firecracker Talk

In the mid-sixties I spoke at a week-long youth retreat at Durley Camp on the outskirts of Greenville, Illinois. My goal was to challenge the young people to commit their lives to Jesus Christ. The theme of the week was, "Are you a disciple or a dud?"

To assist me in holding their attention, I used an "M-80"—the mother of all firecrackers. One "salute" would rock the area with the boom of a canon.

To the best of my recollection, I held up the M-80 on the first night and then placed it on a metal plate on top of the podium where all could see it clearly. I promised I'd be lighting it sometime during my series of talks.

And then I said, "In fact, why don't I light it right now?" I got out a match, struck it, and acted as though I would light the fuse. A bit of pandemonium occurred as those in the first few rows leaned back and covered their ears. A few sought relocation to a safer place. Anxious murmurs surged through the crowd.

Of course I didn't light it then and eventually the place returned to normal. Nor did I light the M-80 the next night or the next. Throughout the week, anticipation mounted as I drew out a match and playfully considered whether or not to light the fuse.

I believe M-80 firecrackers are illegal today. The same is likely true of the famed cherry bomb. These and other Fourth-of-July ear-splitters have caused too many injuries to allow lawmakers to sit by idly.

My first experience with these powerful crackers dates back to my preteen years when I used a portion of my paper route funds to send away for a packet of fireworks. In fact, several of us kids waited each year for the catalogue to arrive and we'd study the pages to find the best deal. I can't be certain of this, but I think we used an address for delivery where parental detection was unlikely.

It's amazing to look back and realize that we could order such things through the mail. And it's even more amazing that we could set these "bombs" off without breaking a law.

One time I wanted to see what would happen if I combined the explosive powder of several firecrackers in an empty baking soda can. I was 12 or 13 at the time. I carefully unwrapped the outer paper and emptied the contents of a dozen regular firecrackers into the can. Then I took the can outside onto the back porch. Two sides of the small wooden porch were open so I felt it was reasonably safe. Oh, I should mention that I was home alone at the time.

I placed the can in the middle of the floor and took out a match from the box. Standing back, I struck the match and tossed it toward the can of gunpowder. Missed. I moved in for a closer shot. This time the match went out before it reached the can.

The third time would work. I leaned over and dropped the lit match directly into the can. BOOM!

I thought I was dead; but dead people don't scream and I was definitely screaming. I checked out my head and limbs and then ran to the bathroom to look in the mirror. My eyebrows were gone! I still had a face.

A neighbor called from the back door, "Are you okay?" I called back, "Yes, I'm okay."

I am reminded of a proverb: "He who digs a pit will fall into it, and a stone will come back upon him who starts it rolling."

Playing with temptation is like messing around with a homemade bomb. The whole thing can blow up in your face. That's why the Bible clearly teaches us to treat temptation like the plague.

I can recall other episodes from my youth that involved firecrackers. Some I'm still trying to forget. Yet in spite of several years of serious "firecracking," neither I nor my friends suffered any lasting ill-effects. This is a credit, I think, to the prayers of our parents and to the protective care of the Lord.

My final session with the young people at Durley Camp was well attended, to say the least. The front rows were occupied by thrill-seeking guys. Everyone was ready for the speaker to keep his promise.

I began my message by taking out the M-80 and setting it on the plate. I said the hour had come; the moment of truth was at hand. I took out a match and after teasing the teens with pretended reticence, I lit the fuse. Faces contorted with fear.

Gasps filled the air. The tough guys in front winced in unison. Camp leaders tallied the cost of a new podium. I accentuated the moment by stepping back and covering my ears.

And then...and then...phzzzzz. I had removed the powder from the M-80 and all it did was fizzle on the plate.

Then I looked out on the teens and drilled home my question, "Are you a disciple or a dud?" My message centered on Paul's passion to follow Christ as related in Philippians 3.

We can look like a Christian and act like a Christian and fool people around us. But it's what's inside that counts. Paul told Timothy to avoid those who hold the form of religion but deny its power. They are phonies, counterfeits, duds. Like an empty M-80, they fizzle in the face of fire.

I urged them to be true followers of Christ and to give their lives to his kingdom. I said something like, "Don't fritter away your lives as fizzling firecrackers. Give yourself to Christ and make your life count for him. Be single-minded. Be real. Be a power-packed disciple.

Chapter 32

Dining On the Ridge

I don't know which of us originated the idea—Spencer or me—but when it came into our conversation, it took on a life of its own. Soon we were checking the calendar and making plans to take our wives on a dinner date different from anything they had ever experienced.

We told them to dress casually and be ready to go at 4 p.m. "Where are we going?" Sandy asked. "Never mind," I said. "Just be ready on time."

Earlier that day, Spencer and I packed the back of my Ford Aerostar van with all manner of food and equipment and covered it with a blanket to keep our surprise a secret. Later, Sandy and I drove to Queen Anne Hill to get Spencer and Karen. An aura of excitement filled the van as we drove down the hill to Interstate 5, and then as we merged onto Interstate 90 and headed east across Lake Washington on the floating bridge.

The women chattered away in the middle seat, taking stabs at possible destinations. When we passed the turnoffs to Bellevue, they revised their guesses to an exotic restaurant in Issaquah. Still we drove east and again the speculations changed. "Did you miss the turnoff?" queried Karen. "I don't know of any good places to eat in North Bend."

By the time we started up toward Snoqualmie Pass, they were beside themselves with bewilderment. Where in the world could we possibly be going? Surely not all the way to Ellensburg; that's another fifty miles!

I drove on, suppressing a grin. Spencer made a few comments like, "Did you ladies bring sleeping bags?"

Near Ellensburg we turned south toward Manastash Ridge. Were we all going to climb the ridge? Is this just a big joke before going into Ellensburg for dinner?

I turned right on Manastash Road and headed into the canyon. They were fit to be tied. What is going on?!

A few miles later, I turned left onto a one-lane dirt road and crossed Manastash Creek on a very unstable bridge. I shifted into low and began the arduous climb up a narrow and rocky Jeep-type road. The chatter from the middle seat subsided. An occasional gasp reached my ears.

Slowly I maneuvered the van up the twisty road, more fitting for goats than a fairly new Aerostar. I wondered if I'd live to regret this escapade.

Finally we broke out on top and drove eastward toward the crest of Manastash Ridge. I steered to a level spot near the edge and stopped. "Everybody out," I instructed. Then Spencer and I told the women to "take a hike" and do some exploring while we fixed dinner.

We unloaded the food, table, chairs, stove, and other gear and set to work. Spencer is a terrific cook and he was quite happy to do the honors. I set the table with linen, silver, goblets, flowers, and whatever else we brought.

The weather was absolutely perfect and the view out over the Kittitas Valley took your breath away. To the northwest, Stuart Mountain stood against the horizon with elegance and majesty.

With Mozart streaming from the stereo, and the sparkling cider and shrimp cocktails chilled and ready, we called for the guests of honor to join us.

I cannot begin to describe the pleasure we experienced as we sat there alone on the rim of this ridge looking out on the most incredible scenery, enjoying a five-course meal featuring filet mignon and a sumptuous dessert.

Halfway through the meal a hiker suddenly popped over the edge of the ridge. He had climbed straight up and nearly crashed into our table after clearing the summit. As he stumbled past gasping for air and quizzically gazing at us with confused eyes, I had the presence of mind to ask one simple question: "Pardon me, sir, do you happen to have any Grey Poupon?"

While he continued on his way without a word, we enjoyed a good laugh. What a grand time we had that night on Manastash Ridge.

As I look back on that special meal with my wife and friends, I'm reminded of Psalm 23 where we read of the Good Shepherd preparing a table before us. I also think of the time Jesus prepared breakfast for his disciples on the beach.

God surprises us at times when we least expect it. Just when we think we are on the edge of a precipice, exposed to the elements of fear and discouragement, he greets us with a meal of encouragement and hope.

Sometimes he takes us to "unknown" places where we are led further and higher, where the view of his handiwork is more awesome, and the refreshment from his hand more delectable.

Just when we need it, Jesus says, "I've prepared a special table for you. Come and have something to eat."

Chapter 33

Laughter On The Lawn

M y first glimpse of the competition unnerves me—a multitude of sleek bodies representing nearly every age. I scan the scene hoping to find at least one specimen in worse shape than me. No luck.

I turn to my wife in horror. She gives me her most understanding look. The kids jabber away: "Win the race, Daddy. Win the race, Daddy."

I open the car door slowly and step into the sweltering heat. It must be 110 degrees and the humidity at least 99 percent.

Bidding farewell to my little fan club, I walk tentatively toward the runners. I feel every eye beholding my new shoes, new socks, new shorts, new shirt, and new head band.

One hundred negative thoughts race through my mind as I maneuver through the cross-country teams, veteran running stars, out-of-town marathon junkies, and spirited young people bouncing up and down eager to begin.

I sign in at the card table and receive a number. My hands tremble as I pin the piece of paper to my shirt.

My first official foot race. I wonder why it took me 37 years to do this. Maybe I should wait another 37 years. I begin to wish I had done more jogging to prepare. I wish I had lost 30 pounds. I wish I had…

But it was only a week ago that I decided to go down to the Chamber of Commerce and register to run in this, the annual two-mile race celebrating the founding of our town, Warsaw, Indiana.

Some of the runners do stretches and calisthenics near the starting line. Others sprint up and down the road. I stand perfectly still, not wanting to waste one milligram of energy.

I notice an ambulance nearby. It will follow us, I learn, to pick up any casualties. The thought consoles me.

Time to line up. We bunch together ready for the gun to sound. I squeeze in at the front. At least I'll be in the lead for the first few steps of the race.

The course will take us one block west, one block south, and then we will turn left for the long run into the middle of town where the crowds await. Another series of left turns will bring us to the finish line at the courthouse square.

Bang!

I lurch forward. Seconds later I'm looking at 90 percent of the runners in front of me. Reaching the first corner I start my turn and catch a glimpse of the pack disappearing around the next corner. It's the last time I see them.

I wonder what pace I can run and still finish. Perhaps I'm starting too slow. I speed up. No, that's too fast. I slow down.

A panting sound behind me brings hope. At least I'm not last. I determine to keep ahead of that noise.

Gasping and swimming in sweat I reach the halfway mark. My body curses me. I think about the ambulance. A side alley looks inviting.

But I press on, pushed by the heavy panting behind.

Just then I hear a question measured out in great gasps of agony. "Why," my pursuer asks, "are we doing this?"

The question plagues me the rest of the race. I sift through a list of reasons. None of them rings a bell.

I pass clowns and floats and marching units waiting to begin the parade which follows the race. Yogi the Bear dances alongside me for a few yards. Not funny.

Now I can see people lining the curbs, leaning out to see who the final runners are. Salt runs into my eyes. It burns.

Just when I need it most I hear a little voice calling, "Daddy, Daddy." I glance to the left and see my two preschoolers waving wildly. Mommy oozes with empathy.

Six blocks to go. A runner in front of me slows his pace. The gap closes and I come beside him. I sputter an encouraging word. Though the roadway is level, he mumbles something about going up hill.

We round two corners and head for the courthouse. All I can see through the blur is a mass of people. It spurs me on. I floor the accelerator. Nothing happens.

Finally, I notice the finish line pass beneath my feet. I gasp wildly for air. My knees buckle.

A nice Red Cross lady takes my arm and hands me a cup of cold juice. I stagger to a shady spot on the courthouse lawn.

I collapse, delirious with joy. I laugh and laugh.

Two applications present themselves. First, I think of the hectic pace of life and our vain pursuits. We can get caught up in things that seem so very important at the moment, but lose their meaning over time. We can allow hobbies to possess us and frivolous goals to absorb our energies.

When our conscience asks, "Why are you doing this?" we just keep on running.

If we are able to extricate ourselves from those time-consuming, energy-sapping, self-absorbing involvements we may feel enormous relief. And yes, we may even laugh on the lawn of life as we celebrate freedom from the tyranny of the urgent. We can now devote ourselves to more worthy pursuits.

The other application comes from the Apostle Paul who said something about finishing the race and keeping the faith. We are in the arena of life and the hope of heaven lies before us. Christ calls us into the race and energizes us with his Spirit. We run against forces of evil and toward the finish line where Christ our Lord is waiting with a crown of righteousness.

Sometimes the sweltering temperature of temptation and the poor conditioning of our souls cause us to stumble and stagger. But then we see the crowd of witnesses and view the finish line ahead. We hear the encouraging words of other believers. We take heart and keep going.

By God's grace we will eventually see the finish line pass under our feet and receive the everlasting cup of refreshment from the Giver of Eternal Life. We will tumble onto the lawn of Heaven and laugh with holy hilarity.

Other Books by the Author

Saga of the Red Truck
(Life Lessons From Here and There)

Hikes, Flights, and Lookout Stories
(Life Lessons From High Places)

For information about these and other publications by G. Roger Schoenhals, visit www.papathree.com. Or contact him directly at roger@papathree.com.

Order Information

REDEMPTION
PRESS

To order additional copies of this book, please visit
www.redemption-press.com.
Also available on Amazon.com and BarnesandNoble.com
Or by calling toll free 1-844-2REDEEM.